Walther Ziegler

Buddha
in 60 Minutes

Translated by
Alexander Reynolds

My thanks go to Rudolf Aichner for his tireless critical editing; Silke Ruthenberg for the fine graphics; Lydia Pointvogl, Eva Amberger, Christiane Hüttner, and Dr. Martin Engler for their excellent work as manuscript readers and sub-editors; Prof. Guntram Knapp, who first inspired me with enthusiasm for philosophy; and Angela Schumitz, who handled in the most professional manner, as chief editorial reader, the production of both the German and the English editions of this series of books.

My special thanks go to my translator

Dr Alexander Reynolds.

Himself a philosopher, he not only translated the original German text into English with great care and precision but also, in passages where this was required in order to ensure clear understanding, supplemented this text with certain formulations adapted specifically to the needs of English-language readers.

Just as the great ocean has but one taste, the taste of salt, so too this dharma and discipline has but one taste, the taste of salvation.[1]

Bibliographic Information held by the German National Library: The details of the original German edition of this publication are held by the German National Library as part of the German National Bibliography; detailed bibliographical data can be found online at www.dnb.de.

© 2021 Dr Walther Ziegler
1st Edition November 2021
Jacket design and graphic design for the whole book: Silke Ruthenberg, making use of illustrations by:
Raphael Bräsecke, Creactive – Studio for Advertising, Comics & Illustrations
© JackF - Fotolia.com (image-frames)
© Valerie Potapova - Fotolia.com (image-frames)
© Svetlana Gryankina - Fotolia.com (speech-balloons)

Printed and published by:
BoD - Books on Demand, Norderstedt
ISBN 9-783-7543-5135-2.

Contents

The Buddha's Great Discovery

The Buddha (560-480 BC)[2] counts, along with Confucius, as by far the most significant and influential of the many philosophers and itinerant wise men of the East. For forty-five years he travelled from place to place in north-eastern India and instructed people on how to live rightly. He is considered to be founder of one of the five great world religions. This is all the more astonishing because the Buddha never claimed, during his own lifetime, to be a prophet. Unlike Mohammed, Moses or Jesus, he promised human beings no sort of afterlife in heaven or in Paradise. Most importantly, he did not believe in God. He also looked very sceptically on the numerous minor godheads who composed the Hindu religion dominant in his time and place. Such ideas, he claimed, are based on mere chance or arbitrary human invention. In his famous parable of "the blind men and the elephant"[3] he compares the high priests of India, the so-called Brahmins, with blind men, who describe their various godheads in the same way as men deprived of sight would describe an elephant. Many years ago, so ran the tale that Buddha recounted to his monks, a king had had several men blind from birth brought into his palace and placed, standing, around an elephant:

Then the king went to the blind men and asked them: 'Tell me, blind men, what is an elephant like?'[4]

The first blind man assured the king that the elephant was like a winnowing basket, since the part of the elephant he had been next to was the big folded cavity of its ear; another said it was like a ploughshare, since the part he had touched was the tusk; another, who had touched the huge torso of the elephant, said it was like a storeroom; another, who had touched the elephant's huge foot, said it was like a milestone; and yet another, who had been placed nearest its tail, said an elephant was like a brush. Each blind man, in other words, described a different part or aspect of the elephant. Nevertheless, a violent argument blew up between them about the elephant's true nature. No different, taught the Buddha, was the situation as regards the supposed truths spoken by the Brahmins and the ascetics about the various gods:

> Even so, monks, are the wanderers of other sects blind and sightless, and thus they become quarrelsome, disputatious and wrangling, (having grasped only a part).[5]

The essential thing, however, is to grasp the whole. It is, for example, wrong, argued Buddha, to invent various gods to preside over different parts or aspects of the world, i.e. a god of health, of fertility, of wisdom, of good fortune at harvest-time or in war, and yet another god responsible for the bringing into being of the world. The Buddha rejected the account of a Creator God named Brahma lying at the root of everything, generally accepted at the time, as firmly as he did the Hindu doctrine of an eternal cycle of re-incarnation and of the immortality of the individual soul. He rejected with especial vehemence the Brahmin religious practice of winning the favour of the gods through the sacrifice of animals.

If we compare it to the ideas generally shared by his contemporaries, the core notion taught by the Buddha is so sober and so radical a one that it is amazing that anyone at all was able to understand what he was teaching. Because for the Buddha the highest goal for Man consists in passing into the state of "nirvana", which means being once and for all "extinguished" as an individual human being. He recommends to his monks and to all those who undertake to join and follow him

[...] The stilling of all formations, the relinquishing of all attachments, the destruction of craving, dispassion, cessation, and extinction (nirvana).[6]

"Extinction" is indeed the literal translation of "nirvana". This state called "nirvana", or sometimes "nibbana", in the ancient Indian languages Sanskrit and Pali is that redeeming final form which a human being can attain once he has come to recognize the meaning of life in all its implications:

The purpose of liberation is nirvana.[7]

The Buddha himself needed many years in order to decipher the meaning of life and to attain to the dimension of nirvana. He was born under the name Siddhartha Gautama as the noble son of a well-respected warrior prince and raised in the royal palace. At the age of twenty-six he left the sheltered and pampered world he had hitherto known and began to roam around India as a "sramana" or "houseless one". He lived on the alms that he begged and attached himself to various brahmin masters and ascetics. But neither the doctrines that he learned from these men nor such ascetic practices as prolonged fasting brought him closer to the goal he was aiming for. It was only after six years of fruitless efforts of this kind that he was able, away from men in the solitude of the natural world, to achieve his redeeming knowledge. Sitting alone under a fig tree, the Buddha discovered his "Four Noble Truths".

Ever since that day these four truths have formed the core of Buddhist teachings. They are of overwhelming clarity and simplicity. Firstly, life means suffering. Secondly, this suffering has a cause. Thirdly, this cause can be removed. And fourthly, there is a specific path which leads to this removal:

[...] When my knowledge and vision of these Four Noble Truths [...] was thoroughly purified in this way, then I claimed to have awakened to the unsurpassed perfect enlightenment in this world [...][8]

The first noble truth at which the Buddha arrived concerns the existence of suffering. It is a truth that it is hardly possible to dispute, since it consists simply in the recognition that every human life is, in basic principle, overshadowed by the painful experiences of growing old, getting sick, dying, and the loss of near and dear ones:

Ageing is suffering, illness is suffering, death is suffering [...], separation from what is pleasing is suffering [...] In brief, the [...] aggregates subject to clinging are suffering.[9]

No anti-ageing programme nor any makeover can free us permanently from the effects of passing time. Nor can anything prevent our losing those who have become dear to us. But instead of trying hopelessly to resist this, argues the Buddha, we need to take a closer look at the emergence and the causes of this suffering. It is here that the second of the Four Noble Truths comes into play: the question as to the causes. The causes of suffering, argues the Buddha, are, in the end, just our own desires for youth, health, immunity from the ravages of time, and personal happiness. But our suffering from these things is something which arises from the fact that we perceive and feel the fulfilment or lack of fulfilment of these desires through our senses and reflectively refer this fulfilment or non-fulfilment back onto our consciousness of being a "self". As soon as we cease to do this, so runs the Buddha's third "Noble Truth", suffering too will cease. The fourth "Noble Truth" then describes the specific way, the famous "Eightfold Path", which we need to travel in order to arrive at this point. This is why the Buddha can say:

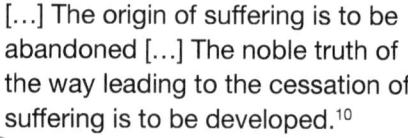

[...] The origin of suffering is to be abandoned [...] The noble truth of the way leading to the cessation of suffering is to be developed.[10]

In that fourth of the "Four Noble Truths" which is also often cited as the "Eightfold Path" the Buddha describes for us in detail how we can progress step by step to the point where are able to ourselves liberate ourselves from suffering. Our "liberation" in this case, however, is, very significantly, not brought about by any God, any Redeemer, or anyone else who "grants us absolution". Nor do we find in Buddhism any "original sin", any "Last Judgment", or any punishing and rewarding God judging us at the end of our lives. It is we ourselves alone who must, by our own efforts, free ourselves from suffering. It is true, indeed, that this freeing of ourselves demands, as its final step, a complete overcoming of the sense of being a "self" and of anything in the world of the feelings or of the intellect's being traceable back to such a "self" or an "I". It is only with this final step that we reach the enlightening dimension of nirvana, as the realization of the fourth and final truth. Buddha describes his own "awakening" in the following terms:

> Being myself subject to birth, ageing, sickness, death, suffering and defilement, true knowledge arose in me and I attained [...] nirvana, the cessation from all doing.[11]

This "arising of true knowledge" in the former Prince Gautama also explains the name that was his from this point on. Buddha means, in the ancient Indian language Sanskrit, "the enlightened one" or, more literally, "the awakened one". For this reason, after his discovery of the Four Noble Truths, which he first announced to the world in the deer park in Benares, Gautama was no longer addressed by his birth name but rather as "the Buddha" or "the Awoken One". The central moment of this awakening was the nirvana experience.

One could say that whoever has understood the concept of nirvana, i.e. the goal set by the fourth noble truth, has also understood the Buddha's central idea. But precisely herein lies the great challenge. The concept of nirvana and all that the Buddha associates with it is, for our Western form of thinking characterized by logic and its principle of logical exclusion, not at all easy to understand. As already mentioned, "nirvana", translated literally, means "to be extinguished". And in fact what is at stake here, for the Buddha, is indeed the "snuffing out" of the self, of the senses, of thought itself, the dissolution of the "I" into the cosmos, into a realm extending far beyond any individual perception of self.

But this "being extinguished" or "snuffing out" are

things which are not so easy to define with any precision. It is a matter neither simply of a state of death or of total non-being, as one might think at first glance, nor of a persisting state of living being. In the binary logic of the Western mind there are always only two possibilities: either something is so or it is not so; either something has a certain quality or it doesn't. To say that both statements are true at once is "illogical" and therefore impossible.

For this reason "nirvana" was, for a long time, translated into European languages as "nothingness", i.e. as a privative thing forming the logical opposite to "something-ness". Consequently, Buddhism became labelled as a nihilism, the goal of which was just a dissolution into nothingness. But this understanding of nirvana covers only a part of its original meaning. The concept "nirvana" does indeed, on the one hand, describe a "nothingness" in the sense of a state of non-being, insofar as, in entering into this state, we leave behind us our sense of self, our feelings, our thinking, and even the very possibility of relating things back to an individual "I". On the other hand, however, nirvana is not a total nothingness or non-being in the sense of a biological death.

What, then, does "passing into the state of nirvana" mean concretely? Are we, when in this state, still "there" or not? Can that meditating person who succeeds thereby in freeing himself completely from his singularity, his awareness of being a "self", still be said to be "alive"? Is he still a subject capable of "knowing", or has he given up, along with his subjectivity, also all possible basis for perception and for memory?

The Buddha discovers, and recounts back to us, the fascinating possibility that one might achieve and experience nirvana even before death, i.e. that one might free oneself for certain periods both from every need and desire and also from the feeling of oneself as an individual self and then, after this profound spiritual experience, return into everyday life. If we succeed, the Buddha goes on to suggest, in achieving this experience of a "snuffing out" of our perception of time and space and of our consciousness of self, then this can serve to remove for us all that is weighty and oppressive in the challenges posed by life and the inevitability of death:

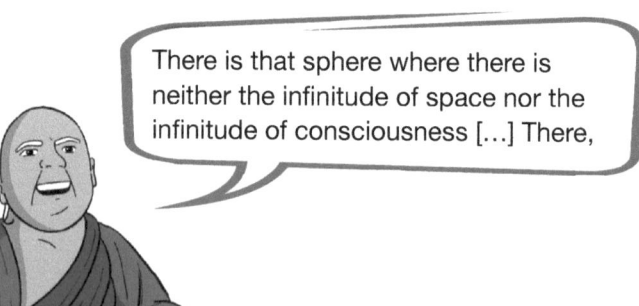

There is that sphere where there is neither the infinitude of space nor the infinitude of consciousness [...] There,

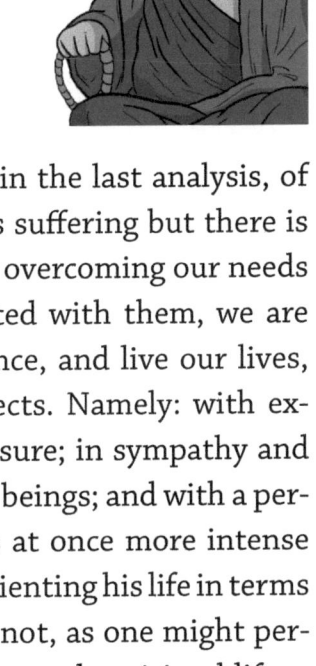

there is neither coming nor going [...]
This, just this, is the end of stress.[12]

The Buddha's key thought is, in the last analysis, of captivating clarity. Life means suffering but there is a way out of this suffering. By overcoming our needs and the individuality associated with them, we are able to experience our existence, and live our lives, anew above all in three respects. Namely: with existential calmness and composure; in sympathy and connection with other human beings; and with a perception of the world which is at once more intense and more fully "present". By orienting his life in terms of nirvana the Buddhist does not, as one might perhaps imagine he would, lead a purely spiritual life, a life turned away from life in the usual sense. Rather, he acquires, precisely through this new perspective, an unclouded and attentive attitude to all that is going on around him:

[Such a one] when going forward or backward, is aware of what he is doing. In looking forward or back he is aware of what he is doing. In eating, drinking, chewing and savouring he is aware of what he is doing. In speaking or in staying silent he is aware of what he is doing.[13]

From this, argues the Buddha, we can derive a basic guideline for the way we approach other human beings and our relation to the world in general:

Monks, a monk should be mindful and clearly aware, this is our charge to you![14]

The Buddha shows us, in his famous "Eightfold Path", how we can attain, step by step, this "mindful and clearly aware" attitude to life and thus achieve a liberation from all dependences.

But is he really still a philosopher in the true sense? Does the doctrine he teaches not rest rather upon what must be called a spiritual experience? It was, indeed, through meditation, or through "looking down into himself", that the Buddha arrived at his key idea of "the Four Noble Truths". Looked at this way, it may well be the case that only those can understand the Buddha's doctrine who have themselves undergone such an experience. Nevertheless, even for all those other people, certainly the great majority, who have not succeeded in achieving this, it is surely worthwhile to follow at least some distance this famous path of the Buddha and to try to come to terms with the philosophy it involves.

The Buddha's key idea is after all, once it is clearly formulated, possible to grasp in rational terms and can also be examined in respect of its usefulness. Are his four great truths really true? Is the "Eightfold Path" really a path we can travel? And if so, what sort of orientation does it give to our ethical action? And: does he not, with his critique of our selfishness and of our restless desire to appropriate the entire world, force us to confront what is currently Mankind's greatest problem?

The Buddha's Central Idea

The Awakening – How Siddhartha Became the Buddha

The Buddha's life has, at first glance, the air of a fairy tale. He was born in Northern India as Prince Siddhartha Gautama, son of King Suddhodana Gautama.[15] The life which seemed to be set out for him was one of wealth, luxury and royal power. But already before his birth his mother Maya had a prophetic dream. In this dream, a white elephant appeared to the pregnant queen and told her that the child she was bearing would one day be a great religious leader. Her husband, King Suddhodana, was deeply disturbed by this dream because he had had quite different plans for his unborn son. The prince was certainly not to be raised to concern himself with spiritual things but rather trained in matters of war and conquest, so as to one day be able to take over his father's throne. When the queen, just a few days after the child's birth, died, the king had the young prince locked up in the palace. Completely cut off from the outside world, he was raised by a nurse and numerous servants and trained principally in the use of weapons.

The grounds of the palace in which Prince Siddhartha grew up were full of exotic plants and animals. Several lotus pools with blue, white and red lotuses were specially constructed just for him. Everywhere he went, night and day, servants held a white parasol over his head, so that his flesh was never touched by heat, cold, dust or dew. A marriage was arranged for him at age sixteen and his beautiful wife soon gave him a child. The young prince, then, lacked for nothing. Nevertheless, he still felt, against the will of his father, the desire to see the world outside the palace walls.

He began secretly to have himself driven outside the palace walls in his coach, exploring the world around it in all directions of the compass. The story goes that, in these four excursions out of the palace, to the north, east, south and west in turn, he saw what are still known as the "Four Sights": that of a sick man, an old man, a dying man and an ascetic. These sights made clear to him that the world he had been living in in the palace had been a world of illusion and he resolved, from then on, to seek the truth. He bade farewell to his wife and child, left all his power and property behind him, and rode out alone into the world where, after six years of seeking and searching full of privations, he finally attained enlightenment.

So runs the legend. The real Buddha, or "historical Buddha"[16], however, was not really a prince and his father was not really a king. He was descended, indeed, from the Gautama family, and thus from the Indian warrior caste, the so-called Sakya clan; but his father was in fact only the administrator of a region, a post he was appointed to by the more powerful ruler King Kosola. The written sources call the father a "raja", a word which can mean both regent of a district and king within an hereditary monarchy.

Most likely it was this ambiguity of the word that lent credibility to the later descriptions of the Buddha as "the son of a king". It is surely also the case that the Buddha's parents' home was no palace but rather just a clay construction perhaps rather larger than those generally lived in at that time and place. Finally, it is unlikely that he had any horses. But these details, reconstructed by historians, do not in the end much affect the core content of the legend. It could indeed be established that he came from a noble family and that he was married at sixteen to the Sakya maiden Yasodhara, who bore him a son. Indeed, it is almost certain that he had several wives, as was normal in that society. He himself recalls:

> I know of no body, no voice, no scent, no taste, no touch, which can so captivate and bind the thought of a man as can the body, voice, scent, taste, touch of a woman.[17]

During his excursions into the outside world, however, Siddhartha learned about the hardness of life outside the sheltering walls of his parental home. Already in early manhood he began to reflect upon the world of pleasure and luxury he had known until then and to question it:

> It became clear to me: those things which give us joy and happiness we call in the world 'enjoyment'. But that the world is ephemeral, full of suffering and subject to change: this is the world's misery.[18]

And Siddhartha recognized that no enjoyment, however great, really lasts for long. Like everything in the world, it is ephemeral and fugacious. From this point on, he became preoccupied by the question of whether there is something that transcends this law of change and fugacity. He resolved to leave his parental home and go to search for this thing. His father consented, very reluctantly, to allow him to go on his way, something which he might well not have agreed to if Siddhartha's son had not already been born, so that the family had a male heir after all, even without Siddhartha:

A black-haired young man endowed with the blessing of youth, in the prime of life, though my mother and father wished otherwise and wept with tearful faces, I shaved off my hair and beard, put on the yellow robe, and went forth from the home life into homelessness.[19]

For the whole of the rest of his life the Buddha now moved from place to place as a "sramana", or so-called "houseless one", begging for alms in order to live. One must bear in mind, of course, that these "houseless ones" were very much more respected in the India of those days than are beggars in our great cities today. The "houseless" were welcomed, and given nourishment, in all the villages and cities of the Indian sub-continent. This was due in part to the fact that there were no mass media in those days and itinerant beggars coming from far away could often tell the inhabitants of the towns and villages they arrived in exciting tales of events in distant regions. The "houseless" often also helped the villagers in various practical ways: the farmers with weather forecasts; the sick with their healing arts; sinners with prescriptions for penance and salvation; warriors with spells which guided their weapons or protected them from injury. The "sramanas", then, included soothsayers and magicians along with teachers of techniques of salvation, healers, philosophers and ascetics. Despite the great differences between these people, however, what they all had in common was that they had decided to forego their positions within the caste system and thereby also all property and all family life.

Siddhartha initially attached himself to two preachers of salvation among the "sramanas". But he soon rejected the doctrines preached by these two men. He continued to wander, at one point attempting, together with five other ascetics, to achieve inspiration through a strict regime of fasting. The five men agreed among themselves that whichever of them first attained to the truth through his ascetic practices would reveal this truth to the others. Siddhartha followed the regime most strictly and consistently, which made him an object of admiration for the others:

> Because of eating so little my ribs jutted out as gaunt as the crazy rafters of an old roofless barn [...] Because of eating so little if I urinated

> or defecated I fell over on my face there. Because of eating so little, if I tried to ease my body by rubbing my limbs with my hands, the hair, rotted at its roots, fell from my body as I rubbed.[20]

But these extreme ascetic practices put Siddhartha's life increasingly in danger. He clearly saw that he was going to die if he continued down this path. Finally, he conceded that

> By such conduct, by such practice, by such performance of austerities I did not attain any superhuman states, any distinction in knowledge and vision worthy of the noble ones.[21]

And he asks himself the question:

> Could there be some other path than this to awakening?[22]

Siddhartha came to recognize, then, that neither a total asceticism nor that satisfaction of every wish, however luxurious, which he had known in his parents' house could really lead a person to deeper knowledge. So, just as suddenly as he had broken with and abandoned the luxurious life of his parental home, he now broke with and abandoned his extreme asceticism and resolved to try to travel, in future, a "middle way":

There are [...] two extremes (of behaviour) [...]: the pursuit of sensual happiness in sensual pleasures [...] and the pursuit of self-mortification [...] Without veering toward either of these extremes [...] the Middle Way [...] leads to peace, to direct knowledge, to enlightenment.[23]

From this point on, Siddhartha began to eat and sleep as much as his body and his health required. The five companions who had admired him so much for the extremity of his fasting and self-mortification were bitterly disappointed in him, and so Siddhartha moved on alone. His search for enlightenment continued for six more years. He wandered on through the entire valley of the Ganges until in the vicinity of Uruvela, today the small city of Bodhgaya, he finally achieved the goal he had been seeking:

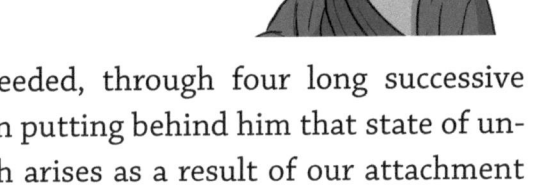

There I saw an agreeable piece of ground, a delightful grove with a clear-flowing river with pleasant, smooth banks and nearby a village for alms resort. And I sat down there thinking: "This will serve for striving".[24]

He then succeeded, through four long successive meditations, in putting behind him that state of un-knowing which arises as a result of our attachment to the world:

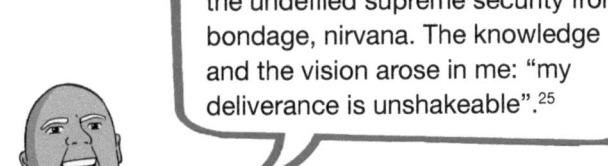

Being myself subject to birth [...] to ageing [...] to death [...] to defilement, and having understood the danger in what is subject to defilement [...], I attained the undefiled supreme security from bondage, nirvana. The knowledge and the vision arose in me: "my deliverance is unshakeable".[25]

Siddhartha Gautama thus became, at the age of thirty-five, the Buddha, the "Enlightened One" or, more literally translated, the "Awoken One". Tradition has it that this occurred under a fig tree in the first night of the full moon in the month of Vesakha, i.e. according to European chronology in the April of the year 528 BC. This day in April is still the Buddhist world's most important holiday and the fig tree has been honoured ever since, in Buddhist cultures, as the "tree of wisdom".

The First of the Four Noble Truths: Life Means Suffering

After having undergone his experience of enlightenment under the fig tree, the Buddha sought out once again the five ascetics who had been his former companions in fasting and other self-mortifications. At first they refused to keep company with him, since he had deviated from their path of strict asceticism:

But the closer I drew to the five "sramanas" the less they were able to hold to their fixed intention.[26]

Right away on hearing the Buddha's first words these ascetics sensed that their former companion had returned to them transformed and inspired. In the deer park Ispatana in the vicinity of Benares he delivered to these former companions the famous discourse about the Four Noble Truths which was later to gain worldwide recognition as the key idea of Buddhism. The tradition has it that the Buddha, with this first didactic discourse, "set in motion the Wheel of the Dharma". These Four Noble Truths are: knowledge, cause, end and removal of suffering. Great development is given to the concept of each in turn in the Buddha's later speeches and discourses. *The first of the Four Noble Truths* is easy to understand. Human life is automatically bound up with suffering. It begins with the strain and stress involved in our birth and continues unrelentingly from there:

> Birth is suffering, ageing is suffering, illness is suffering, death is suffering, [...] separation from what is pleasing is suffering [...] In brief, the five aggregates (that bind to the world) are suffering.[27]

That these "aggregates binding to the world" are experienced by human beings as a source of suffering is a contention that is hardly to be disputed. They clearly form part of our existential condition. Each of us must, sooner or later, have the painful experience of being subject to sickness, accidents, old age and bodily decay. And each of us also knows what it means to lose near and dear ones as the years roll on. This is why the Buddha can write:

This Noble Truth of suffering is to be fully understood.[28]

One might, of course, object here that the Buddha entirely overlooks the fact that life also, on the other hand, contains many joyful experiences and moments of pleasure. The Buddha does not, indeed, deny the existence of such moments; but he points out that they are of short duration. True happiness, however, must be something enduring. And in fact we do always try to draw out our moments of happiness, and our wishes, and make them last. Thus couples who have fallen in love, for example, swear, in the marriage ceremony, to stay together "till death us do part". But things very often turn out differently. Because, as the Buddha insists, no joy that life provides to us can ever be held onto for long or its possession be made secure forever. On the contrary, the greater the number of things and human beings we love, the more keenly will we experience their fugacity and their loss:

> Who loves a hundred things knows a hundred different kinds of suffering. Who loves ninety, ten or five things knows ninety, ten or five kinds of suffering. Whatever suffering there may be in the world, that suffering will always have arisen through the love of some thing.[29]

But human beings do not suffer just from the loss of beloved people or beloved things. They also suffer from not being able to get things which they strongly desire. Such is the case with couples, for example, unable to have children; with artists whose works fail to be recognized; with bachelors and spinsters who never find their ideal partner; trained actors who can get no role and therefore cannot live out their passion; and generally with all those people whose private or professional aims are never realized:

Not to obtain what one wants is suffering (dukkha).[30]

We also suffer, the Buddha points out, from the worry that we might in future lose what we already possess, be it our beloved partner, our child, our job, our health, or our youth. Life, then, means suffering. Upon this first basic truth the Buddha now lets a second follow.

The Second of the Four Noble Truths: The Cause of Suffering

The *second of the Four Noble Truths* reveals to us the deeper ground of, or reason for, our suffering. In order to understand this cause the Buddha recommends that we adopt an unexpected, radical change of perspective. The deeper cause of our suffering, the Buddha argues, lies not in the unexpected misfortunes which befall us and in the inconstancy of all that we possess in the world but rather in the way in which we deal with these facts of our existence. That we eventually must experience old age, sickness and death is something which arises, in the last analysis, simply from the natural laws of this existence. The real problem here is the attitude which we adopt in the face of these inevitable natural laws. We tend to look on personal losses, advancing age, and death as things unjustly inflicted upon us, as insults and torments that we undergo. The Buddha, however, teaches us a better way of looking at things. A good example of this is the tale told of the woman and the three grains of wheat.

A woman desires a child for many years and finally bears one. But the baby dies soon after it is born.

The woman refuses to accept what has happened and persuades herself that the child is not dead, just sick, and must somehow be made well. Clutching the dead child to her breast, she goes around the village asking the inhabitants for help. These latter send her to the Buddha, who happens just at that time to be in the neighbouring village. And the Buddha does indeed promise to help her. He tells her that in order for him to do this all she has to do is bring him a few grains of wheat from three different houses in her village in which no one has died. All the households of the village are, of course, in principle willing to give the poor woman a few grains of wheat for this purpose. But all of them must also admit that they cannot claim to be houses in which no one has died. Many people, indeed, had died in all of them; many more than were now living in each and many of the householders break down in tears when the woman makes her request, remembering all their own dead. Encountering, then, so many cases of losses suffered by others, the woman begins to understand that what has befallen her is in fact just one small case of the universal law which dictates that all that lives must die. She is then able to make peace with her child's death and give it a proper burial, after which she returns to the Buddha and becomes one of his followers on the path toward full awakening.

This change of perspective from a purely subjectively experienced individual suffering to a recognition of the objectivity of universal laws is the first step to recognizing the causes of the suffering of the world. A second step can now be taken which involves grasping the individual conditions which alone make it possible that we refer this suffering back to ourselves as an individual or personal matter. It is here that there comes into play the Buddha's famous doctrine of Paticcasamuppada, or "dependent co-arising":

From the arising of this comes the arising of that.[31]

The Buddha poses the fundamental question: what condition needs to apply in order for the impression of something like suffering to arise in me? What must be the case in order for ageing, for example, or sickness and death to also be the case? His answer runs:

Whatever suffering arises, all that is rooted in desire, has desire as its source.[32]

If we do not desire something, we do not suffer from achieving it or from losing it once it is achieved. If, for example, we do not desire our own youth, then losing youth by growing old will matter not at all to us. But for the Buddha this does not go far enough. He probes deeper than this, going on to ask: what condition must apply in order for us to be able to desire at all?

(These are the foundations out of which desire arises) [...] Forms cognizable by the eye that are wished for, desired, agreeable and likeable, connected with

sensual desire and provocative of lust.
(Likewise) sounds cognizable by the ear
[…] odours cognizable by the nose […]
Flavours cognizable by the tongue […]
and tangibles cognizable by the body.[33]

This too is plausible. Desire becomes possible only if we have already perceived the desired thing through our senses. This is the case whether it is a matter of smelling the scent of a good meal, seeing a person we find attractive, or hearing an enticing melody. Sense-impressions, in other words, are the necessary precondition for all desire. But what is it that conditions these sense-impressions? What is it that must be present in order for us to be able to process sense-impressions at all?

From name and form as a requisite condition come the six sense-media.[34]

Sense-impressions, argues the Buddha, are only as intensive as they are because we are able, thanks to our consciousness, to assign and attach these sense-impressions to certain "names and forms". For example, we would be completely overwhelmed by the many sounds, shouts, scraps of speech, and images suddenly flashing out of nowhere in the average cinema film, and these sounds and images would soon disintegrate in our memory and dissolve without a trace, if we could not assign them to some unifying and connecting story or idea, i.e. organize them in terms of specific names, forms and colours and thereby give them a sense. It is in this way that we come to understand these otherwise meaningless sounds and images as forming something "beautiful", "ugly", "dramatic", "romantic" and so on. Thus we organize an image of two young people, the touching of their lips, the sunset behind them and the music in the background into the form "kiss"; or an image of a red dress, hair blowing in the wind, brown eyes, a curvaceous figure, and an enchanting voice into the form "beautiful woman".

But what is it that conditions, in turn, our ability to assign sense-impressions in this way to specific names and figures? The precondition for any such assigning is the activity of a consciousness. This consciousness creates these names and figures through its action of referring all that our senses perceive back to something which we consider an "I" or a "self". Thus, for example, the form "beautiful woman" is only such a form for us, i.e. for our individual consciousness of self. But what is, to go a step farther, the precondition for us doing this and relating those things to which we have assigned name and form back to ourselves as the individual consciousness that we are? What, indeed, is the precondition for our having an individual consciousness at all? This precondition consists in what the Buddha calls "the fabrications". It should be noted, though, that the word rendered as "fabrications" here might be better rendered as "fabricating forces", since it refers to those forces which make consciousness as an assigning and organizing consciousness and which sustain this latter, for the whole length of the life of a human being, as something which divides the world into "mine" and "yours".

Finally, the Buddha asks about the precondition which must be present if these "fabrications" or "fabricating forces" are themselves to come into being. What is it which brings it about that there arise "fabricating forces" which cause our consciousness to impose names and forms upon all that we perceive through our senses and thereby to awaken in us a desire for the things thus arising: a desire which may be satisfied or remain unsatisfied in each particular case but which will lead necessarily, whatever the case, to suffering?

From ignorance as a requisite condition come fabrications (fabricating forces).[35]

The condition and cause, then, of the arising of these "fabrications", or "fabricating forces", which make up our consciousness is ignorance. Here, clearly, an entirely new dimension enters into play. The factors which we have called "determining" up until now have all been factors that could not be changed or altered. Desire, we have said, emerges out of our sense-perceptions: i.e. out of our hearing, seeing, smelling etc. These sense-perceptions, in their turn, are determined by the giving of names and forms, and this giving of names and forms determined by consciousness, and consciousness finally, determined by what we have called "fabrications" or "fabricating forces". Thus far, the determining factor has in each case been something unalterable. What determines, however, these last-mentioned "fabricating forces" seems, by contrast, to be something that we can alter. The Buddha says that the determining condition of the "fabricating forces" is ignorance, and ignorance can always be replaced by non-ignorance, i.e. by knowledge. It is here, then, that the Buddha's doctrine of "dependent co-arising" acquires its emancipatory impulse. The Buddha himself sums it up as follows:

When this is, that is. From the arising of this comes the arising of that [...] When this isn't, that isn't. From the cessation of this comes the cessation of that.[36]

The essential point of the doctrine of "dependent co-arising" is to be found in the final sentence of the passage just cited: "From the cessation of this comes the cessation of that". This means that if we succeed in interrupting the mechanism formed by the whole sequence of "dependent co-arisings", then no further suffering can arise. That is to say, there falls away the entire chain of factors which lead, in the end, to our desiring things and to our feeling a sense of pain and loss when we fail to acquire or lose them. In short, the entire sequence "ignorance, 'fabricating forces', consciousness, imposing of name and form by consciousness, sense-impressions, desire and suffering" can be interrupted and ended, provided only that we replace ignorance with knowledge. What this means concretely is of enormous significance. This transformation of ignorance into true knowledge, and the radical consequences of this transformation, is something which the Buddha addresses in the third of his Noble Truths.

The Third of the Four Noble Truths: The Removal of Suffering

The *third of the Four Noble Truths* shows us how we can break out of "dependent co-arising" and leave the cause of suffering behind us. The decisive lever which we need to use in order to do this consists in the transformation of ignorance into knowledge.

From the cessation of ignorance comes the cessation of fabrications. From the cessation of fabrications comes the cessation of

consciousness. From the cessation of consciousness comes the cessation of name and form. From the cessation of name and form comes the cessation of the six

sense-media. From the cessation of the six sense media comes the cessation of contact. From the cessation of contact comes

the cessation of feeling. From the cessation of feeling comes the cessation of craving. From the cessation of craving comes the cessation of clinging/sustenance.

From the cessation of clinging/sustenance comes the cessation of becoming. From the cessation of becoming comes the cessation of birth. From the cessation of birth,

then ageing and death, sorrow, lamentation, pain, distress and despair all cease. Such is the cessation of this entire mass of suffering and stress.[37]

In the centuries after his death the Buddha's doctrine of "dependent co-arising" was often represented in diagrammatic form by Buddhist monks.

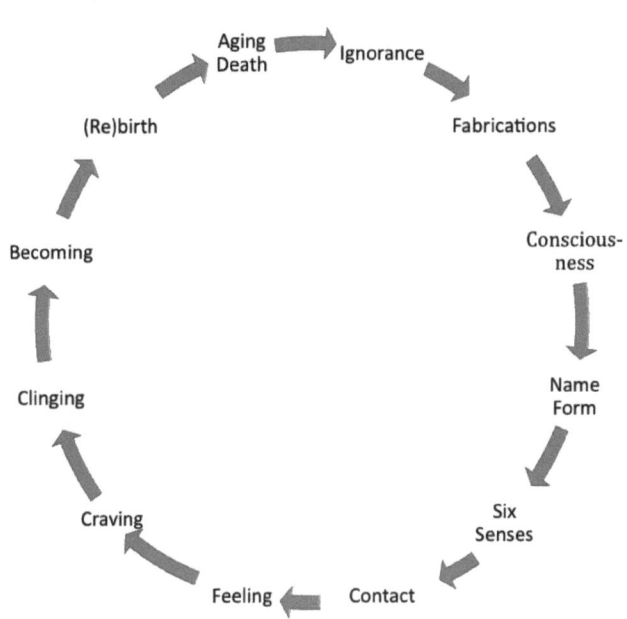

What is the Buddha trying to say to us with his talk of our being freed of all these determining factors and what they determine? And what does it mean that at the end of all this there will no more becoming and no more birth, no more ageing and no more death?

In a first step, what is important to the Buddha is that we come to recognize that all our violent desire, our wishes and our passions are not insurmountable real factors but rather only consequences of an attitude which arises out of ignorance. They ensue from a kind of blindness or, as Buddha also describes it, an "impurity" whereby the "fabrications" and the forces which fabricate them are held to be things unalterable and a whole life, therefore, is spent sustaining and serving them. That their "arising" is indeed a "dependent co-arising" is completely overlooked:

> This generation delights in worldliness, rejoices in worldliness. It is hard for such a generation to see the truth [...] namely, that of dependent co-arising.[38]

Someone, however, who possesses the knowledge which teaches that all that to which we feel attached, all that which delights us, consists only in false attachments to the world and that, in addition to this, our very consciousness of ourself as an "I" is a false consciousness will be able to free himself from these attachments, will be able to overcome his own desire and thereby overcome suffering. Because for the Buddha not just the "fabrications" but also our own ego, that is to say, our own idea of our own self, our self-consciousness or self-awareness, are all illusions which must be overcome. And one can indeed overcome these illusions by ceasing to blindly subject oneself to "dependent co-arising":

But the instructed noble disciple does not regard form as self, nor feeling as self, nor volitional formations as self, nor consciousness as self [...] He is freed from form, freed from feeling, freed from volitional formations, freed from consciousness. He

is freed from birth, ageing, and death, [...] freed from sorrow, lamentation and [...] despair.[39]

Here we see just how radical are the insights which follow from an understanding of "dependent co-arising". It is not only our desire that must be recognized to have "arisen co-dependently" and thus to be, in the end, something illusory and unreal. We must also recognize this to be the case of that consciousness of being a "self" to which we refer back all that we know and believe to be:

Suppose [...] a dog tied up on a leash was bound to a strong post or pillar. If it walks, sits or lies down, it walks, sits and lies down close to that pillar. [...] So too, the uninstructed worldling regards form, feeling, perception, consciousness thus: 'This is mine, this I am, this is myself'[40]

There is, the Buddha argues, really neither a consciousness which recognizes itself as a "self" nor a "self" which exists as a conscious being in the world. The experience of the "non-I", or "non-self", or in other words the attaining of a condition in which all thinking in terms of distinctions and separations, and every relation of the "other" back to the "self", is overcome, belongs to the very core of the "nirvana" experience. This can, indeed, initially be something difficult to understand. Perhaps the best point for trying to begin to grasp the idea here is the Buddha's contention that everything that we perceive, however great or small, arises from a construction or "fabrication" which is not in the external world but rather emerges within our own interior being. This applies, argues the Buddha, to our perception of an attractive person, of a beautiful work of art, or of the universe as a whole:

And what [...] is the all? The eye and forms, the ear and sounds, the nose and odours, the tongue and tastes, the body and tactile objects, the mind and mental phenomena.[41]

With these words the Buddha tells us quite unmistakably that the entire world around us, even the universe itself, comes to be only through ourselves, specifically through the perceptions mediated by our sense-organs. But this need not be the end of it. Whoever has recognized that our perceptions are a matter of "dependent co-arising" also knows that:

> There is an escape from this
> whole field of perception.[42]

And this applies not just to our perception of the whole world external to us but also to our perception of our own selves. One of the Buddha's own monks found that he had great difficulty accepting this idea. He could not help thinking that one had, in the end, surely to assume that some sort of "subject" underlay all touching and feeling. Otherwise, he asked: "Who touches? Who feels?" The Buddha replied:

> (This is) not a valid question. If I should say:
> 'One makes contact', in that case this would
> be a valid question. Since I do not speak
> thus, […] the valid answer is: 'With the six
> sense bases as condition, contact (comes
> to be); with contact as condition, feeling.[43]

The Buddha, then simply repudiates, in basic principle, all questions as to a "subject", arguing that such questions lead in the wrong direction and down a completely false track. One ought rather to try to adopt an objective viewpoint and to understand perception generally as a process in which even selfhood proves to be merely a determined and fabricated phenomenon. That is to say: proves to be a mere appearance or illusion which can and must be seen through. We human beings, in other words, do not merely mentally create a world around ourselves but even create these very selves. All the ideas which we have of ourselves and of the world arise within the tiny space of our own heads. Therefore, it is also within this tiny space that the key to liberation lies:

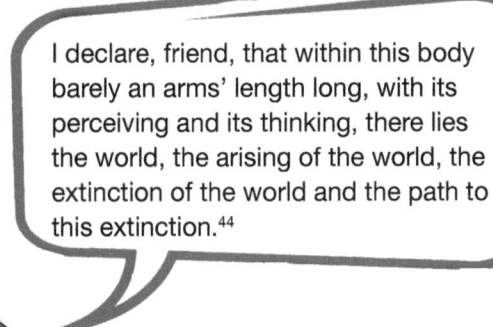

I declare, friend, that within this body barely an arms' length long, with its perceiving and its thinking, there lies the world, the arising of the world, the extinction of the world and the path to this extinction.[44]

The Buddha urges us, then, to see the truth about our own subjective role and part, mediated by our perceiving and thinking, in the arising and coming to be of the world we know, to annihilate or "extinguish" this part of ours in the construction of the lived world, and to choose in its stead to strike out on the path to "non-selfhood". Whoever succeeds in doing this, he says, will see the world with new eyes:

(The awoken man) regards what is seen, heard, sensed, cognized, encountered, sought, mentally pondered thus: 'This is not mine, this I am not, this is not myself'.[45]

In this way, we can adopt an attitude of complete equanimity and overcome suffering altogether. It is no longer circumstances which decide whether we shall be happy or not. We no longer even perceive such things as ageing and death. We are thus liberated from every sort of dependence. The Buddha describes his own liberation as

The stilling of all formations [...] The destruction of craving, dispassion, cessation.[46]

He recounts to his monks his own experience of nirvana in the most gripping terms:

Searching, I attained the deathless, sorrowless, supreme security from bondage, nirvana. The

knowledge and vision arose in me: 'my deliverance is unshakeable; this is my last birth; now there is no renewal of being.'[47]

This radical liberation from all perceptions of the thinking apparatus and the sense organs makes possible that "nirvana experience" which lies beyond our accustomed world of "dependent co-arising" This experience is an experience from which all pain, suffering and even death are absent, since it involves no consciousness of any "I" which might become aware of these phenomena in relating them back to itself and thereby begin to be afraid of them. Nirvana, literally translated: "extinguishing", means a leaving behind of all relation to an "I" and thus of all those "fabricating forces" which lead to the accumulation of "karma". This Sanskrit term "karma" designates an action or effect which proves to have consequences either for the life one is presently living or for the lives that one will live after one's rebirth. It is, indeed, only through the attainment of nirvana that all the "fabricating forces" leading to the accumulation of karma are brought to cease and be still, so that no rebirth occurs.

The Buddha also mentions at this point that this liberation from suffering and from the causes of suffering is something which does not apply just to our own existence and to the span of time covered by this existence. The awakening which takes place in the "nirvana experience" means, in the last analysis,

also a liberation from suffering for all the living beings who will follow us and for all following generations. If we succeed in ceasing to cling to the illusion
of an "I"-consciousness and even in freeing ourselves
from all clinging to life itself, this means that we will
leave behind us no negative energies: energies which
might conceivably have caused later generations to
make the errors we have made. It is here that there
comes into play the Buddha's vision of a chain of
births and rebirths whereby those who have not yet
attained true knowledge are driven from existence to
existence:

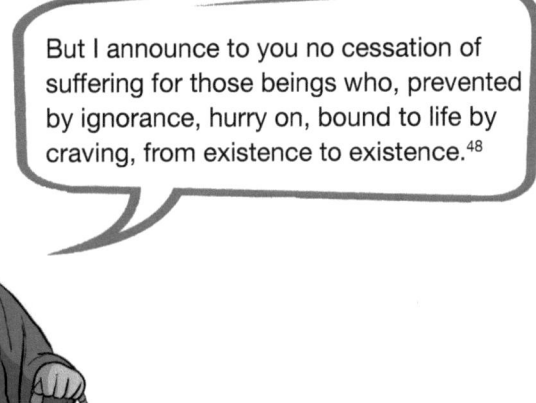

But I announce to you no cessation of suffering for those beings who, prevented by ignorance, hurry on, bound to life by craving, from existence to existence.[48]

It is, however, the contrary announcement and
promise to this that the Buddha makes to those who
have "awoken" and attained to knowledge:

There is that dimension, monks [...] where there is neither coming, nor going, nor staying [...]: an unborn, unbecome, unmade, unfabricated.[49]

In order to understand the significance of rebirth and reincarnation in the Buddha's thought one must bear in mind the historical situation in ancient India. According to the Hindu religious vision widely accepted at the time every human being possesses, deep in his inner nature, an immortal soul ("atman") which reincarnates, after the death of the particular individual's body, in some new being, be it a man or woman, an animal, or even a god. The Buddha himself, after his awakening under the fig tree, had a vision which at first sight strongly recalls this Hindu idea:

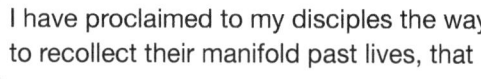

I have proclaimed to my disciples the way to recollect their manifold past lives, that is, one birth, two births, three births, four births, five births, ten births, twenty births [...], a hundred births, a thousand births, ten thousand births, many aeons of world-contraction, many aeons of world-expansion.[50]

During his meditation the Buddha also saw pass before his mind's eye all the other living beings who had ever been on earth and who had left their karma behind them there:

Thus, with a divine, purified eye (I saw) beings passing away and reappearing, inferior and superior, fair and ugly, fortunate and unfortunate and (I understood) how beings pass on according to their actions.[51]

This, the Buddha's doctrine of reincarnation certainly gives rise to many questions which continue even today to be objects of controversy among scholars of Buddhism. On the one hand, the Buddha describes here a law-like process or sequence whereby souls "pass on" into new bodies in accordance with their good or bad actions. On the other hand, however, he sees in this no personal reincarnation, no persistence of an individual soul or of a personal consciousness. For the Buddha, the entire personality of a human being, including his consciousness, dies with this human being's death. In this regard, his doctrine of reincarnation is different from many other Indian doctrines of salvation.

In Buddhism we see neither, as we do in the Jain religion, some such unchanging being as the god Jiva who is said to participate in all past and future beings and to live in these latter forever, nor, as in the Upanishads, an unchanging individual soul, an "atman", which leaves the body after death and passes into another body. The Buddha's doctrine of "anatta" designates, in sharp contrast to the notion of "atman", the non-existence of any permanent or unchanging soul or "self". He calls the Hindu ideas of an eternal, immortal soul "utterly and completely foolish":

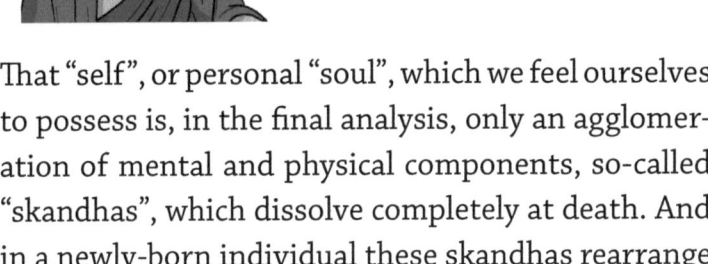

'After death I shall be permanent, everlasting, eternal, not subject to change; I shall endure as long as eternity': would this not be an utterly and completely foolish teaching?[52]

That "self", or personal "soul", which we feel ourselves to possess is, in the final analysis, only an agglomeration of mental and physical components, so-called "skandhas", which dissolve completely at death. And in a newly-born individual these skandhas rearrange themselves in a completely new way.

The energies of those who have previously lived, however, insofar as these latter never achieved awakening, remain, the Buddha argues, in the world and may produce effects in, and do harm to, some new existence. Such energies would take the form, for example, of wars, or catastrophes unleashed by individual dictators: legacies which can leave their mark on later generations without the members of these generations being actual reincarnations of the dictators in question into whom the immortal souls of these latter have passed. Later Buddhists compared this impersonal passing of karma from one generation to another with the lighting of one candle by another's flame. If one takes a long narrow candle made of blue wax and uses its flame to light a short thick candle made of red wax the flame, indeed, is passed from one to the other but the two candles remain things completely distinct and different from one another. Alternately, the image of the torchbearer is also used here. When a torchbearer passes on his torch to another, the energy remains a constant but the personalities stay distinct. On one occasion when a monk wrongly assumed that the Buddha's teaching did indeed evoke an immortal individual consciousness which passed over onto the next person after death, with the deeds of previous lives being reckoned to the new one, the Buddha corrected him in the strongest terms:

Misguided man, to whom have you ever known me to teach the Dharma in that way? Misguided man, in many discourses have I not stated

consciousness to be dependently arisen, since without a condition there is no origination of consciousness? But you, misguided man, have misrepresented us by your wrong grasp and [...] stored up much demerit.[53]

The Buddha's doctrine of reincarnation, however, only plays a role in the Four Noble Truths to the extent that that path of knowledge and awakening pointed up by the Buddha signifies a twofold liberation: in the first place the liberation of the individual human being from the suffering which he undergoes during the span of his own life; in the second place the general liberation from suffering which occurs from the elimination of all karma in all possible rebirths, the extinction of all negative energies also for coming generations:

The knowledge and vision arose in me: 'Unshakeable is the liberation of my mind. This is my last birth. Now there is no more renewed existence.[54]

To sum up, then: the first Noble Truth describes suffering, the second suffering's cause, the third the elimination of suffering through the acquiring of knowledge of its "co-dependent arising". As soon as we leave behind us, in mastering the third Noble Truth, those illusions which are desires, perceptions and our sense itself of being a "self", we are in a position to free ourselves from suffering. Since this liberation and the attainment of not-being-a-self go hand in hand with full "awakening" and the experience of nirvana, the key question arises: how, concretely, do we go about achieving this experience? The answer to this question is given by the *fourth and last of the Four Noble Truths* .

The Fourth of the Four Noble Truths: The Eightfold Path

What the Buddha himself called the "Eightfold Path" has remained a core element of the Buddhist doctrine in all of Buddhism's many schools and tendencies. It contains instruction on many matters relating to the theory of knowledge, the practice of meditation and ethics. This is why the Buddha calls it a "way", translated more concretely a "path", which prepares us for, and leads us step by step to, "awakening":

And what [...] is this Middle Way [...] which gives rise to vision, which leads to nirvana? It is the noble Eightfold Path; that is, right view, right intention, right speech, right action, right livelihood, right effort, right mindfulness, right concentration.[55]

These eight steps to "awakening" can be assigned to three different fields of activity or phases of development. In the first phase, that of right view and intention, it is a matter of gaining basic insight into the doctrine; in the second phase a matter of the ethical attitude which arises from this insight: i.e. of right speaking, acting and a corresponding style of life; there then follows, in the third phase, the final great step to inward "concentration" or "samadhi". Inward concentration is the life-attitude which hones and perfects attention and the practice of meditation with a view to awakening in the nirvana experience. All these eight steps, however, are a matter not of a mere series of skills which are to be sequentially learned but rather of the slow unfolding of inherent virtues which – and this is the important thing for the Buddha – must in the end all be lived and applied at the same time.

1.	Right view	Insight
2.	Right intention	
3.	Right speech	Ethics
4.	Right action	
5.	Right livelihood	
6.	Right effort	Inward Concentration
7.	Right mindfulness	
8.	Right concentration	

The "right view" mentioned in the first step consists simply in our coming to understand that all our relations with and references to the world are fugacious and ephemeral, that is to say, productive only of suffering. Nothing really provides lasting happiness: neither a relation to a beloved partner, a mother, a child, nor our youth, health, beauty, success or material goods. And from the inevitable loss of these things there ensues suffering. In order to prevent this pre-programmed suffering we must recognize and overcome its source: namely, our clinging to life as a desire which arose only through "dependent co-arising". The first step on the Eightfold Path, then, requires that we recognize and understand the Four Noble Truths at least theoretically.

What distinguishes the "right intention" which forms the second step is that it enables us to recognize, through the knowledge of the Four Noble Truths, the great evils committed by the mind that is misled. We now know that greed, envy, anger and other bad thoughts arise only through a false relating of everything back to a "self" and through an unreflective attachment to sense-perceptions and their temptations. On this second step of the path we attempt already to replace a selfish and egoistic mentality with a mentality of composure and equanimity.

The third step's "right speech" is distinguished by a complete renunciation of all lying and unconsidered words, that is to say, an end to all insulting or degrading of people, something which can very easily happen in everyday life.

The fourth step's "right action" demands ethically exemplary behaviour according to the basic principles laid down by the Buddha. First and foremost among these is the foreswearing of all stealing, robbing and adultery, as well as of the tormenting or killing of any living beings.

The "right livelihood" mentioned as the fifth step follows directly from the preceding principles of "right speech" and "right action". Because this fifth step unmistakably demands that the theory of ethical thought and action be translated point by point into actual practice in life. Thus, the principle of right speech would require, in practice, that one never, be it either in one's private relations or in one's capacity as trader, businessman, artisan or political ruler, attempt to fool or cheat other people. The ethical command of "right action" requires avoiding the killing of both human beings and animals and this must be reflected in the whole of life, for example also in professional life. On this fifth step of the Eightfold Path the individual has empathy with all living beings, human or animal:

> He abstains from killing living beings. With rod and weapon laid aside, gently and kindly, he abides compassionate to all living beings.[56]

This applied not only to the Buddha's own monks and pupils. The Buddha's doctrine also forbade laymen to trade in weapons, in living beings, in meat, in alcoholic beverages, and in poisons. For this reason, such professions as butcher, bird-catcher, hunter, fisherman, warder, soldier or arms-dealer were not to be engaged in. Still today, these professions are practiced in Buddhist nations rather by Christians or Muslims.[57] Furthermore, a vegetarian diet is followed as far as possible in these countries and drugs seldom used.

With regard to the proper way of living the Buddha demands "the observance of the Five Rules". Firstly, never deliberately to kill or injure any living being; secondly, to commit no theft; thirdly, to lead a morally pure life, i.e. avoid sexual excesses and marital infidelity; fourthly, to tell no lies nor use any crude language; fifthly, not to cloud and obscure one's awareness by use of drugs.

The decisive thing here is that the true path in life is one that can be achieved only through one's own efforts. Impure thoughts, words and deeds must be overcome by our own selves alone. This requires a striving for purity which can in no case be replaced by any external action or practice, such as animal sacrifices or ritual purifications. The Buddha fundamentally rejected both the ritual bathing in rivers which was widespread in India in those days and the equally widespread practice of animal sacrifice. On one occasion, for example, the Buddha posed to a Brahmin who was on his way to "purify" himself in the holy river Bahuka the following very direct question:

Why, brahmin, go to the Bahuka river? What can the Bahuka river do? [...] A fool may there forever bathe, yet will not purify dark deeds.[58]

Even if he should bathe like a fool in the river forever, argues the Buddha, he would never be able spiritually to wash himself clean. The Buddha urged the brahmin to follow, instead of this, the Five Rules he proposed. It was, he said, no supposedly holy river water coming from distant sources that would provide him with purification but only a plunging into his own personal moral actions, a plunging which could be performed without any long journey to any traditionally holy place:

> It is here, brahmin, that you should bathe. One fair in act, one pure in heart, brings his virtue to perfection.[59]

As he does so often, the Buddha here takes up an existentialist stance. No higher power, no God, nor any gods decide, swayed by sacrifices or ritual purifications, the issue of our moral purity. We are guilty, if we are guilty, vis-à-vis supernatural powers but rather only vis-à-vis ourselves. In contrast to the Hindu beliefs prevalent in his time and place, for the Buddha there was no divine court of justice which condemns or acquits us after our death.

The "right effort" evoked as the sixth step requires that we persevere upon the path of the morally good life without ever flagging in our determination. The issue here is tenacity. This may seem to go without saying but this is not in fact the case. Many people make, for example, "New Year's resolutions" but they hold to them only for a short period of time.

Such is the case with many resolutions and decisions. Mistakes we may make and offence we may give to other people can sometimes lead to us resolving to change and to pay better attention, in future, to the wellbeing of others. But the decisive thing here is, as the Buddha emphasizes with this sixth step, the sustaining of a "right effort" which will ensure that such resolutions are really put into practice over the longer term. The Buddha required such an effort especially from his own monks.

The "right mindfulness" evoked as the seventh step likewise concerns the actual putting into practice of our resolutions and of our moral stance in general. Because such a practical realization does indeed require, in every life-situation a concentration of the mind. It is, for example, important, both when one is alone and when one is in company, to be mindful of and attentive to one's own feelings, thoughts and actions, and also to recognize the effect of unconscious impulses, deciding whether to allow them free rein or, if one recognizes them to be harmful, to master and control them.

"Mindfulness", however, should not be taken here to mean the strict suppression or repression of any thoughts or feelings which seem unpleasant. It means only that we should deal with these thoughts and feelings in a more enlightened way. In contrast to the "driven" atmosphere of our day-to-day lives, in which all we have in our heads is the next appointment or deadline, "mindfulness" means an attentive lingering in a specific situation, an intensive perception of inner and outer circumstances. Mindfulness of the "inner" ensures that we remain aware of the constant flow of our feelings and our states of consciousness and can no longer be overcome or driven by them. It allows us to be completely present in the here and now, neither clinging to the past nor losing ourselves in plans for the future. Floating freely throughout our conscious being, it has a soothing effect both on ourselves and on others. This is all the more true in cases where we find ourselves met with mistrust, anger or hatred. In his famous *Simile of the Saw* the Buddha describes this mindfulness in all its broad implications:

When others address you, their speech may be true or untrue […], gentle or harsh […]. Even if bandits were to sever you savagely limb from limb with a two-handed saw […] (you should say): 'Our minds will remain unaffected and we shall

utter no evil words. We shall abide compassionate for their welfare, with a mind of loving-kindness […] We shall abide pervading the all-encompassing world with a mind

[…] abundant, exalted and immeasurable, without hostility and without ill will.[60]

"Right concentration" as the eighth step forms the final conclusion of the Eightfold Path to "awakening", completing and perfecting the other steps through a meditative sinking into contemplation. In the last analysis, indeed, these eight steps are not to be taken

to represent any temporal or substantial sequence but rather all build on one another right from the very start and exert their effects on one another mutually, so that they must all be lived through together at one and the same time. Nevertheless, "samadhi", "right concentration", this eighth and last of the steps on the Eightfold Path leading to "awakening" and thus to the "nirvana experience", inarguably forms a distinct and special element of this Path. Through meditation, or through "sinking into ourselves" as the Sanskrit word "dhyana" might be more literally translated, we are able to actually "experience" what we have already theoretically recognized and understood: for example, the doctrine of the four truths or that of "dependent co-arising". The detaching of ourselves from those desires and perceptions which have arisen "dependently" in this way, along with the overcoming of "I"-consciousness, are then no longer matters of merely theoretical insight or knowledge. They are made concretely present to us in the practice of meditation and their overcoming is made experienceable. But liberation from all attachments, i.e. the experience of nirvana, requires long practice, often years long, and application of the right techniques. It is very far from being a simple process. Through "sinking into ourselves", however, argues the Buddha, we can indeed succeed in freeing ourselves from all illusions of the world and of the self. He describes this condition of radical liberation in the following terms:

Any kind of form whatsoever, whether past, future or present, internal or external, gross or subtle, inferior or superior, far or near,

having seen all consciousness as it really is, (one knows): 'This is not mine, this I am not, this is not myself'. [...] When one knows and sees thus [...] one is peaceful and well liberated.[61]

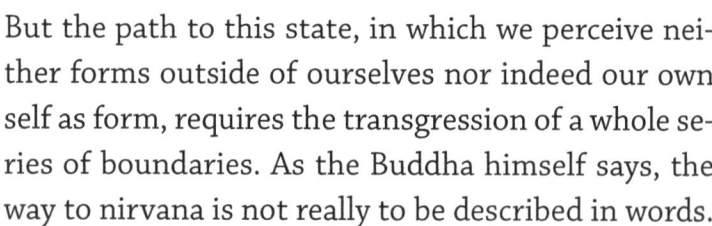

But the path to this state, in which we perceive neither forms outside of ourselves nor indeed our own self as form, requires the transgression of a whole series of boundaries. As the Buddha himself says, the way to nirvana is not really to be described in words.

He nevertheless makes the attempt to do so, describing the various stages of the experience of a meditating individual:

By completely surmounting the base of infinite consciousness, aware that 'there is nothing', (he) enters upon and abides in the base of nothingness [...] Again, by completely surmounting the base of nothingness, he

enters upon and abides in the base of neither-perception-nor-non-perception [...] By completely surmounting the base of neither-perception-nor-non-perception, (he) enters upon and abides in the cessation of consciousness and feeling.[62]

With the passing away of consciousness and feeling suffering from the world is also overcome, since there is now no longer any subjectivity or sense of an "I" to which this suffering might be referred. In short, then, the Buddha's Eightfold Path is a path to salvation. This path aims ultimately at leading us toward overcoming the great illusion that we stand over against the world as a being completely separate from it and from other beings. Through meditation the prison-house of the self can be broken open. Then, our illusory "consciousness of self" will no longer block our way to the truth that is nirvana.

Of What Use is the Buddha's Discovery to Us Today?

The Buddha's Answer to Humanity's Most Important Questions – Beginning and End of the World

The Buddha's ideas were far ahead of his time. The philosopher Karl Jaspers names him, along with Socrates and Confucius, as one of the three great thinkers of the "Axial Age": an age in which there emerged for the first time, on different continents, an entirely new understanding of the world which pointed the way forward for humanity. The Buddha did indeed represent, in almost every respect, views and convictions which anticipate our modern ones: equality between men and women; refusal of class and caste distinctions; refusal also of such archaic practices as burnt offerings or living sacrifices to appease the gods. He criticized particularly sharply the idea widespread among the brahmins of the day that, if one made a sufficient number of sacrifices, one could secure for oneself eternal life and a union with God. None of these brahmins, the Buddha pointed out, had ever seen or met God. Those who preached belief in a monotheistic divinity seemed to him to be like:

> A file of blind men clinging to each other; the first one sees nothing, the middle one sees nothing and the last one sees nothing.[63]

He also compared the man who aspired to enjoy, after his death, a kind of community with God, or who wished to revere some God who was himself immortal, to a man adoring a woman supposed to be the most beautiful in all the world without ever having actually set eyes on this woman or gotten to know her in person:

> (People) might say to him: 'Do you know what caste she belongs to? [...] Her name? [...] Her clan? [...] Her clan? [...] Where she comes from? (To

all these questions) he would say 'no'. [...] Does not the talk of that man turn out to be stupid?[64]

The Buddha was equally critical of magicians, healers and clairvoyants. He even explicitly forbade his own pupils to present themselves as equipped with any sort of magical skill or ability. He himself, moreover, never performed any miracles, even though one of his monks once urged him to do so in order that the Buddhist movement might acquire thereby more prestige. But unlike all the many brahmins, teachers of salvation and prophets who, like himself, passed their years travelling across India teaching and preaching, nothing resembling any "magic" is recorded at any point in the Buddha's life. Whereas tradition tells us that Jesus of Nazareth, for example, performed such marvellous deeds as walking on the water, healing the blind, the deaf, the lame and the leprous, and even bringing the dead back to life, no such miracles are recorded as having been performed by the Buddha. In this respect too, then, he makes a "modern" impression. The Buddha too, indeed, often helped the needy. But the methods he used to do so were, in comparison to Christ's, of a disarmingly pragmatic nature. Thus, for example, he advised a man who could not accept the death of his wife and kept putting off burying her to yield to his impulses and to stay seven more days close to her body. In this way, the ever stronger stink of rotting flesh cured the man of his morbid attachment.

Above all, however, the Buddha was astonishingly pragmatic in the answers he gave to the great questions facing humanity. When he was asked about the beginning and the end of the world he recounted to his astonished audience a dream that he had had the night before. The Buddha had dreamed that one of his students had personally encountered the Creator God Brahma and had asked him about the end of the world:

Where do the four great elements – earth, water, fire, air – cease without remainder?[65]

In the Buddha's dream Brahma, doubtless the best person to address about these matters, answers as follows:

Monk, I am Brahma, Great Brahma, the Conqueror, the Unconquered, the All-Seeing, the All-Powerful, the Lord, the Maker, the Creator, the Ruler, Appointer

and Orderer, Father of All That Have Been and Shall Be.[66]

But this, continued the Buddha, was not enough to satisfy the monk. He repeated his question twice more but received from the Creator God each time only, once again, a long listing of all the divinity's titles and powers. When the monk, insisting, posed the question yet a third time, Brahma looked nervously over his shoulder to see if any other deities were present and perhaps listening and then something very strange occurred:

Then the Great Brahma took the monk by the arm, led him aside and said: 'Monk, these gods believe that there

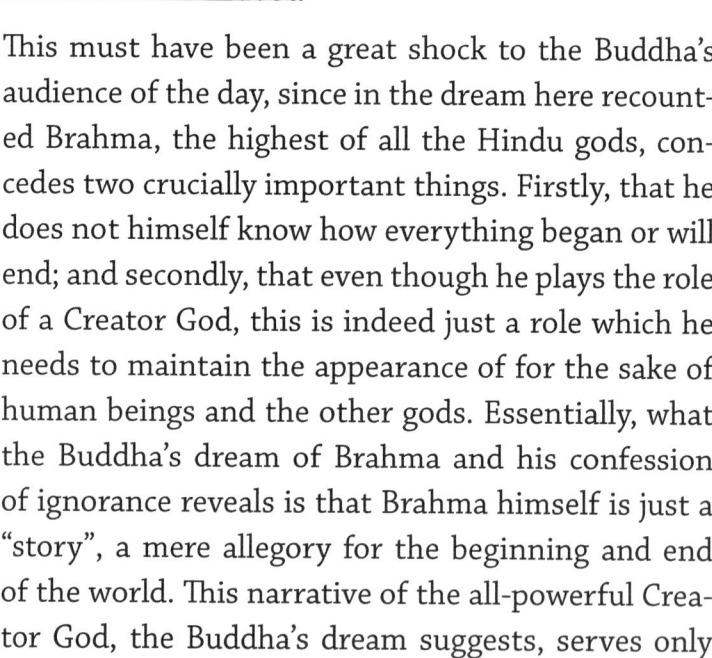

is nothing Brahma does not see, there is nothing he does not know, there is nothing he is unaware of. That is why I did not speak in front of them. But

monk, I don't know where the four great elements cease without remainder.[67]

This must have been a great shock to the Buddha's audience of the day, since in the dream here recounted Brahma, the highest of all the Hindu gods, concedes two crucially important things. Firstly, that he does not himself know how everything began or will end; and secondly, that even though he plays the role of a Creator God, this is indeed just a role which he needs to maintain the appearance of for the sake of human beings and the other gods. Essentially, what the Buddha's dream of Brahma and his confession of ignorance reveals is that Brahma himself is just a "story", a mere allegory for the beginning and end of the world. This narrative of the all-powerful Creator God, the Buddha's dream suggests, serves only to relieve human beings of the burden of having to torment themselves with thoughts of eternity and infinity. It is only someone who has seen through this story as indeed just a story who can attempt to look the truth in the face. Entire galaxies, argues the Buddha, arise, pass away and then arise again just as millions of flowers bloom and fade and then bloom once more, or millions of human beings or animals are born, die and are replaced by others of their kind:

Beyond comprehension [...] are the beginning and the end of this cycle from birth to death and then back to rebirth.[68]

Even, indeed, our own present-day narrative of a "Big Bang" would likely confirm the Buddha in his expressed view that the beginning and end of the universe are "beyond comprehension". This "Big Bang Theory", which currently enjoys wide scientific recognition, proposes that our universe arose some 13.8 billion years ago out of a so-called "singularity", i.e. out of an extremely minimal point of infinite density, and that it continues since then to expand ever farther until, having reached a maximum extension, it begins to contract again and ends in another "Big Bang". These notions of "infinitely high density", "eternal expansion" and "eternal contraction followed by new unfolding" firstly constitute things which are hardly strictly scientifically measurable; secondly, they cannot really be said any longer to represent a truly definitive "beginning" or "end" scenario. To this extent, we may say that the cosmological narrative recognized and predominant in our own day too, namely that of the "Big Bang", recalls and refers back to the Buddha's cosmological narrative characterizing beginning and end of the universe as "beyond comprehension".

Just as the Buddha has, in this dream, a pupil monk of his speak with the Creator God Brahma in order to refute the notion that this latter knows all and is responsible for the beginning and end of the universe, so too is the Buddha himself reported as having spoken on several occasions with the gods, something which acquired for him the title: "Teacher of Men and Gods". He is recorded as having exposed and overcome in argument even Mara, god of death and misfortune. Often in the Buddhist scriptures, the gods appear in the role of supplicants or assistants to the Buddha. For example, we are told that when the Buddha achieved "awakening" under the fig tree he was initially in doubt about whether he would really be able to communicate his Four Noble Truths, the so-called "Dharma", to the world and that it was a god who then personally asked and urged him to do it:

Then the Brahma Sahampati [...] appeared before me [...] and extending his hands in reverential salutation, said:

'Venerable Sir, let the Blessed One teach the Dharma [...] There are beings [...] who are wasting through not hearing the Dharma [...]' Then I listened to Brahma's pleading [...].[69]

On another occasion, when the Buddha had to suffer a downpour of rain lasting several days, he was aided by the nature deity Mucalinda in the form of a snake, who spread his seven heads over him so that they formed a kind of umbrella. This image of the Awoken One in perfect harmony with Nature was later to become a popular motif in Buddhist art.

How are we to understand all this? Did the Buddha himself believe in the gods? Here we must bear in mind that the Buddha lived in a world in which the Hindu deities had been firmly anchored in the minds of men for more than a thousand years. The Buddha had necessarily to deal with this fact. But he did so with a certain playfulness and lightness. He does not deny the existence of the gods but shows up the weaknesses they share with human beings. In the last analysis he makes use of these Hindu gods as symbols and allegories lying fortunately to hand with which he can illustrate certain theses and explanations regarding the world, then going on to use these world-explanations either as foils for his own ideas or as confirmation of them. The Buddha always, indeed, treats the Hindu deities respectfully in his discourses and conversations. But at the same time he plays with them, as if with chess pieces, in order to clarify certain elements of his own thought.

Whether, or to what extent, the Buddha himself believed in the real existence of the Hindu gods are questions that prove, in the end, very hard to answer. One thing is certain, however: he always stresses, in his remarks about the gods, that these latter are all, without exception, subject to death and that they are robbed, by the proclamation of the Buddha's own doctrine, once and for all of the illusion of their own immortality:

The gods, argues the Buddha, are subject to the law of arising and passing away as much as human beings are. They too make mistakes and are mortal. The Buddha even suggests that the special status accorded in the religion of those days to the gods, who were seen as heavenly and infinitely powerful beings, had had the effect of making the gods even more subject to these errors and failings than human beings were. It was even more incumbent, then, the Buddha believed, on the gods than on ordinary human beings to make great efforts to overcome their ignorance and their selfishness. The Buddha, in other words, humanized and secularized the gods, binding them, as it were, into the earthly human community. He leaves no doubt that his doctrine applies to human beings and gods alike.

Can Everyone Follow the Way of the Buddha? The Simile of the Raft

It is, of course, possible in principle that pupils, monks and indeed every human being might follow the same path as did the Buddha and thereby become Buddhas themselves. According to Buddhism's own understanding, a "Buddha", or an "Awoken One", is any person who has, by his own efforts, developed the purity and perfection of his own mind and spirit to such a point that he can achieve nirvana and live free from desire, filled with wisdom and empathy. It is impossible to calculate, using rational criteria, the number of people who might conceivably achieve such a condition. The Buddhist tradition, however, tells us that Buddhahood is achieved only relatively seldom. For this reason, the ages in which a Buddha makes his appearance are called by Buddhists the "Fortunate Ages", the ages in which no Buddha appears the "Dark Ages". In certain countries of the Far East the later Buddha Amitabha is more widely revered than Buddhism's founder, Gautama.

There are today more than three hundred million Buddhists worldwide, above all in Thailand, China, Myanmar, Vietnam and Japan. Buddhism is the fourth largest world religion, after Christianity, Islam and Hinduism. It must be noted, however, that Buddhism has by now split into many different schools and sects, even if all of these latter have their ultimate origin in the inspiration of Gautama under the fig-tree.

One tendency within Buddhism which has remained very close to the Buddha's original "Four Noble Truths" is Hinayana, sometimes also called Theravada, Buddhism. "Theravada" means, literally, "the School of the Oldest" and has its origins in that group of monks who had become Buddha's companions already during the Master's own lifetime. The successors to these monks have thus preserved the Master's teaching almost intact. In the centre of Theravada Buddhism stands the self-liberation of the individual through the experience of nirvana, just as the Buddha had taught:

Whoever, o monks, beholds the Four Noble Truths becomes liberated from feeling, from volitional fabrications, from consciousness of self [...] Thus he experiences salvation from suffering. This is I proclaim to you.[71]

In later years, however, the Buddha began to be perceived no longer as a teacher but as a divine being himself. He began to be worshipped in temples erected for this purpose and prayed to in religious services. Around five centuries after the Buddha's death there emerged the second great school of Buddhist belief which today numbers over two hundred million believers, making it the largest of the Buddhist congregations: namely, Mahayana Buddhism. "Maya" means "large" or "great" and "yana" means "vehicle", so that the word as a whole means "great vehicle". That is to say, the Mahayana Buddhists see their own doctrine, which has expanded the original Buddhist teaching by adding to it the idea of the Buddha being himself a god, as the "Great Vehicle", describing the original doctrine itself, somewhat derogatorily, as the "Small Vehicle", or "Hima-Yana", since the original Buddhists had been concerned only with the individual's personal self-liberation.

In Mahayana Buddhism, by contrast, the highest goal is the liberation and salvation of all beings from suffering. Mahayana Buddhists believe that this can be achieved under the guidance of spiritual teachers called Boddhisatvas, since there is in every human being, from birth on, a certain innate direct access to the Absolute. The Boddhisatvas therefore no longer aim, as the Buddha had, directly at achieving nirvana, since they wish, through a long series of births and rebirths, rather to lead all other beings toward the Absolute. The Buddha is revered here as a sort of spiritually transcendent higher court. The Buddha as a really existing human figure no longer exists in Mahayana Buddhism. His appearance on earth is interpreted as a projection of the Absolute, a mere appearance which the true divine Buddha took on temporarily so as to announce the true doctrine to human beings. But in this way that doctrine of human wisdom taught by the Buddha begins to become indistinguishable from a religion.

There emerges as a sub-form of Mahayana Buddhism a school called Vajrayana Buddhism: the so-called "Diamond Vehicle". This is a form of Buddhism practiced above all in Tibet. Vajrayana Buddhism is opposed on several essential points to the original doctrine of the Buddha. It makes much play of demons and minor gods. Moreover, like the Catholic Church with its bishops, cardinals and Pope, Vajrayana Buddhism displays a strict and elaborate hierarchy in which the priests enjoy great power. At the head of it stands the Dalai Lama, whose power is absolute. Whereas the Pope derives his authority only from being the successor of Saint Peter as bishop of Rome, the Dalai Lama is honoured as a god. He is taken to be the direct incarnation of the Buddha, his name meaning "Oceanic Teacher" or "Ocean of Wisdom".

If we compare it to the elaborate additions and developments which it has undergone in the course of hundreds of years the original teaching of the Buddha stands out in several important respects. It is not a religion; it involves no liturgy, no temples, no priests, no "believers" in the traditional sense. And above all else: the Buddha is no god. And like all good teachers he recommends to his students that, as soon as the time is right, they leave his teaching behind them. It is very important to the Buddha that the students of his doctrine begin, at some point on the road to "awakening", to trust rather in themselves. He makes this clear in his famous simile of the raft. This describes a man standing before a seemingly insurmountable obstacle: a great river which prevents him from pursuing the journey he is on. In order to cross it he makes use of all the materials he can find in order to construct a raft. Once on the other side of the river, he feels very satisfied. He is unwilling to abandon the vehicle which has brought him so far and thinks to himself:

> This raft has been very helpful to me since, supported by it, I got safely across to the far shore. Suppose I were to hoist it on my head or raise it on my shoulder and then go wherever I want.[72]

The idea of taking the useful vehicle along with one may seem at first to be a good idea. But as the Buddha points out, it would certainly soon itself become a hindrance and a burden to the man on his journey. The man should rather, he argues, let go and ask himself:

Suppose I were to set it adrift in the water and then go wherever I want? It is by so doing that the man would do what should be done with the raft.[73]

The Buddha, moreover, leaves no doubt about how this story should be interpreted:

So I have shown you how the Dharma is similar to a raft, being for the purpose of crossing over, not for the purpose of grasping.[74]

Indeed, the Dharma can never be any more than a useful vehicle on the path to "awakening". It can point up the way we must take, just as the footprint of an elephant can reveal to us the general direction we must follow. But the decisive step, the overcoming of the six senses and of the consciousness of the self, must be made by each individual for himself. Clinging to the example of the teacher, or idolizing this latter, can become an obstacle to one's own awakening. One Chinese Zen Buddhist master even went so far as to say: "If you meet the Buddha on the road, kill him. Only then will you achieve liberation and not be bound to things."[75] What is meant here, of course, is the "killing" of the Buddha in the metaphorical sense of a freeing of oneself from him as an overly dominating idol on one's own path to the nirvana experience.

The Buddha himself concedes that, although a certain direction is indicated by the specific items of his teaching, such as the theory of the causes of suffering and of suffering's overcoming, true awakening is a spiritual experience which goes far beyond anything that might be taught in the form of an item of doctrine:

Truly, I have discovered the doctrine which is hard to perceive and to grasp and that cannot be attained through logical thinking.[76]

True "awakening", then, is not to be grasped through the understanding alone. It even escapes exact description through language. Buddha's philosophy in fact is based, besides upon the doctrine of the Four Noble Truths, "dependent co-arising", and the Eightfold Path, above all on the experience of meditation.

A true understanding of the Buddha's key idea of "extinction" is only to be achieved through the "sinking down into oneself", or redeeming practice, of meditation. The Vietnamese Zen master Thich Nhat Hanh, most likely the best-known living Buddhist next to the Dalai Lama himself, has even said that the practice of meditation is the only path that really leads to Buddhism.[77] It is surely this practice of meditation that continues to form, even today, a large part of Buddhism's fascination. Buddhism, indeed, has made, since its birth in India, triumphant progress all around the world. And we have today countless forms and practices of meditation which, originating in Buddhism and in Yoga, have long since grown beyond them. These run from breath- movement- and song-form meditation practices, through various Tantric and other yogic techniques, to the meditative flower-arrangements practiced in Zen Buddhism (Ikebana), tea ceremonies, karate and calligraphy techniques. Below, however, we will present only the techniques proposed by the Buddha himself.

The Secret of Breath-Meditation: Don't Think!

The Buddha himself practiced, all his life, so called "breath meditation". He also recommended to all his pupils and monks, as well as to laypeople, this inward-looking form of concentrated "sinking down into oneself". The Buddha himself achieved awakening under a fig tree in an idyllic rural landscape. But meditation, he taught, can also be practiced simply in an empty room. The only important thing is that one not be disturbed. The key is outward and inward stillness:

A bhikkhu (monk) goes to the forest, or to the root of a tree or to an empty hut, (folds) his legs crosswise (and sets) his body erect [...].[78]

The specific position of the body which the Buddha recommends here is that "lotus position" well-known from many traditional Buddhist images and representations. It is a position which automatically gives to the meditating individual, thanks to the crossed legs and the erect attitude of the upper body, a certain bodily tension which is neither so comfortable as to make him drowsy or so stressful of the muscles as to cause him pain. The arms rest with palms turned upward on the meditating person's legs:

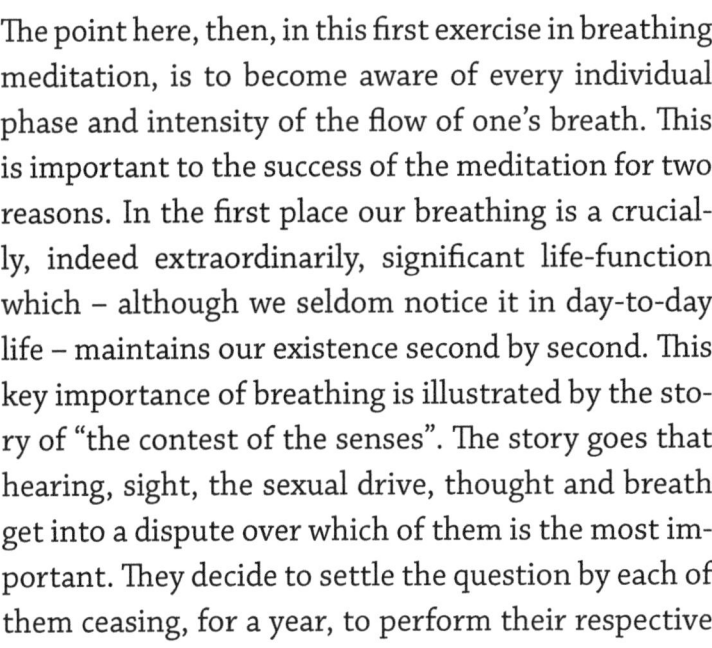

(Having) established mindfulness in front of him, ever mindful he breathes in, ever mindful he breathes out. Breathing in long he understands:

'I breathe in long', or breathing out long he understands: 'I breathe out long'. Breathing in short he understands: 'I breathe in short', or breathing out short he understands: 'I breathe out short'.[79]

The point here, then, in this first exercise in breathing meditation, is to become aware of every individual phase and intensity of the flow of one's breath. This is important to the success of the meditation for two reasons. In the first place our breathing is a crucially, indeed extraordinarily, significant life-function which – although we seldom notice it in day-to-day life – maintains our existence second by second. This key importance of breathing is illustrated by the story of "the contest of the senses". The story goes that hearing, sight, the sexual drive, thought and breath get into a dispute over which of them is the most important. They decide to settle the question by each of them ceasing, for a year, to perform their respective functions. The year without sight leads, as does the year without hearing, to various accidents and injuries. The year without thought naturally gives rise to many serious errors. The sexual drive too, as the bringer of much pleasure, is naturally sorely missed. But life goes on nonetheless. But no sooner has the faculty of breathing suspended its functions than the other senses declare it the victor and beg it to begin to do its essential work once again.

Another important aspect of breathing is that, in contrast to other vitally necessary functions such as the heartbeat or the circulation of the blood, it can be consciously controlled. One can choose to breathe faster or slower or even, for a time, to hold one's breath. Since it is in this way at once something we can control and a process that goes on automatically and independently of us, breathing places us, right at the beginning of any meditation, within our existence's essential field of tension: namely, that of the power, on the one hand, to influence something while on the other hand being surrendered to laws outside ourselves, or in other words being at the same time subject and object in the world. And this is the key thing.

The Buddha sees in the attentive observation of breathing the opportunity to overcome self and subjectivity and to attain an objective dimension of perception liberated from the illusion of the "I". Breath binds us indissolubly to the world. Although at the beginning one may be aware primarily of oneself as the breathing subject, in the course of time one finds oneself dissolving more and more into the process itself of breathing in and out. One becomes aware only of the breath flowing inward and outward, without wanting to change or influence it in any way. The autonomous subjectivity of the breathing person, which had in any case all along been only an illusion, passes into the background and even vanishes.

The next advantage of concentration on breathing consists in its gaining one inner peace. By feeling our breathing we can focus on something which frees us from the everyday sphere of our thoughts. Because a decisive factor, in any case, for the progress of meditation is the letting-go of our reflective consciousness:

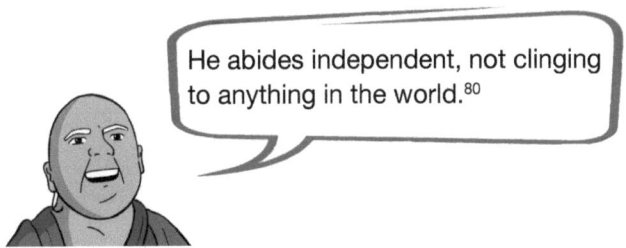

He abides independent, not clinging to anything in the world.[80]

But really things are not quite so simple. Most people do find themselves "clinging to things in the world".

Even when meditating, they have the problem that, right at the start, a flood of thoughts rushes through their heads. This is quite normal, since our brain is programmed to solve problems all day long. Whether crossing the road, working, or going shopping, we always encounter situations in which one experience must be gauged against another. Conclusions must be drawn, strategies developed, and decisions taken in split seconds. It is natural, then, that when, in the peace and isolation of meditation, a certain space arises, this space is immediately filled with thoughts. Like a wound-up watch-spring, our brain cannot stop functioning. It continues to process all that it has absorbed during the day or that it remembers from still farther back. The Buddha recommends that we do not try simply to push aside thoughts that come to us in meditation. He holds that it is permissible to linger with them for a while until we recognize their conditionality, only then pushing them gently out of our minds. The same applies to any feelings that might arise:

When feeling a pleasant feeling a bhikkhu (monk) understands: 'I feel a pleasant feeling'; when feeling a painful feeling he understands: 'I feel a painful feeling'; when feeling a neither-pleasant-nor-painful feeling he understands:

'I feel a neither-pleasant-nor-painful feeling [...] He abides contemplating in feelings their arising factors, or he abides contemplating in feelings their vanishing factors.[81]

The meditating person is advised to proceed with his own body just as he does with his feelings. He should observe it for a while but then simply leave it behind him, as something which has merely "dependently co-arisen". That is to say, he looks on his own body objectively and with equanimity, as a mere agglomeration of material components:

In this body there are head-hairs, body-hairs, nails, teeth, skin, flesh, sinews, bones [...], heart, liver [...]

large intestine, small intestine, contents of the stomach, faeces, bile, phlegm, pus, blood [...], oil of the joints and urine.[82]

The meditating person can leave his body behind him as a form of clinging to the world by making himself aware of the ephemeral nature of all the body's component parts and by, for example, bringing to his mind's eye an image of this body's final resting place:

As though he were to see a corpse thrown aside in a charnel ground [...], disconnected bones, scattered in all directions [...] In this way he abides, contemplating the vanishing factors of the body.[83]

In the same way he recognizes his own "I"-conscious-ness as something subject to "dependent co-arising". He contemplates this "I"-consciousness's ephemeral nature and transcends it through meditation:

By completely surmounting the base of infinite consciousness, aware that 'there is nothing', (he) enters upon and abides in the base of nothingness [...] and by completely surmounting the base of nothingness, (he) enters upon and abides in the base of neither-perception-nor-non-perception.[84]

Once the meditating person has succeeded, then, in leaving behind him his body, his feelings, his con-stantly active thought-processes, and finally that consciousness which distinguishes "self" from "oth-er", he is in a position such that he can reduce and bring to peace and stillness perception as a whole. That is to say, he can cease to smell, see, feel or taste, so that he is finally definitively in the realm of not-thinking and not-perceiving anything at all.

In the final stage of meditation the aim is to bring it about that the meditating person can achieve this without any active effort to do so: that is to say, that he ceases to have to engage in any psychical expenditure in order to prevent the perception, or compel the non-perception, of anything at all. Instead, his aim is now to attain a condition characterized by equanimity and total absence of tension in which he no longer needs to engage in any sort of struggle since he now finds himself once and for all beyond the dimension of perception and non-perception:

By completely surmounting the base of neither-perception-nor-non-perception, the bhikkhu(monk) enters upon and abides in the cessation of perception and feeling […] This bhikkhu is said to have crossed beyond attachment to the world.[85]

This final "crossing beyond attachment to the world" is nirvana, the highest goal of meditation:

The eternal, the unborn and unbecome, the place without suffering or error, the extinction of the bad factors of existence, the cessation of the fabricating forces – this is happiness.[86]

Nirvana and Everyday Life – The "Two Worlds" Problem

The overcoming, then, of weighing, calculating thought is the decisive step on the path leading to the experience of nirvana:

[...] which means the freeing of that which lies beyond all weighing and calculating thought.[87]

It is here that one really gets clearly to see the revolutionary, and indeed for a Western sensibility at first sight quite uncanny, core idea of the Buddha's teaching. The essential thing for the Buddha is precisely this achievement of a state or condition lying "beyond all weighing and calculating thought". But is such a thing even possible? Are we able still to know or experience anything where we pass beyond this accustomed type of thinking? Or must our entire experienceable world come to an end with the end of thinking in words and propositions? Just this was contended, for example, by the logician and philosopher of language Wittgenstein, who argued that there could be, in basic principle, no knowledge outside of the limits of a weighing, judging, language-mediated thought: "the limits of my language are the limits of my world".[88]

Schoolchildren in France and many other countries of the Western world also learn the view of the great rationalist Descartes whereby our weighing, judging thought is something we simply can never "get behind", this thought itself forming the guarantee and the proof of our existence: "I think, therefore I am".[89] I can indeed, argues Descartes, doubt all that I see and feel, since all this could be, as the Buddha puts it, merely a "dependently co-arising" fabrication or illusion; but, at least in the moment of doubting, the doubt itself, i.e. this particular form od weighing, judging thinking, cannot be doubted. It is thought, then, that provides us with an immediate certainty of our existence. Because in the moment in which I doubt something, whether I am right to doubt it or not, it is certain that I, at least, as the doubting mind, exist.

The Buddha, on the other hand, sees this certainty of self which arises in the moment of thinking as a merely apparent self-certainty, a stage of transition to be passed beyond. He would surely have classified Descartes' "I think, therefore I am" as a purely provisional form of the appearance of "dependent co-arising". We can indeed be said to "be", argues the Buddha, in the moment of our straining and stressful thought in "samsara, i.e. in the world of "dependently co-arising" perceptions, but one always has the possibility of overcoming this world and leaving it behind.

With "nirvana" the Buddha reveals to us a horizon of experience which transcends and surmounts the immediately obvious horizon of judgmental thought and of the "I"-consciousness. It is not thought that is the highest form of knowledge; knowledge's highest form is rather a state that has been freed from thought. Thought referring to itself, he argues, is no saving "life-belt" in the search for truth but rather an obstacle in this search. The Buddha would surely have revised Descartes' "I think, therefore I am" to "I think, therefore I am not yet awakened".

Because as long as we continue to cling to judging and distinguishing thought we remain also under the sway of the idea of a thinking "I" which relates all that happens in the world back to itself. The world of the thinking "I" is merely derivative from the perspective of the true world of nirvana, and of only relative reality since it is determined by ignorance. But one is justified in asking: does this "other world" of nirvana really exist?

Buddha argues for it first by using a procedure of logical exclusion. Nirvana must be possible, because otherwise there would be no possible escape from the normal world, so that he himself would never have escaped from it:

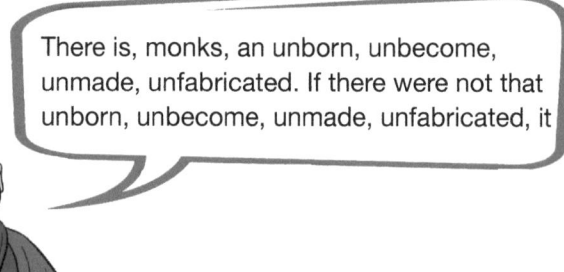

There is, monks, an unborn, unbecome, unmade, unfabricated. If there were not that unborn, unbecome, unmade, unfabricated, it

it would not be the case that escape from the born, become, made, fabricated could be discerned.[90]

The Buddha then attempts to describe to us more exactly the world of nirvana or this "other place" here evoked:

There is a place in which there is neither earth, nor water, nor fire, nor wind, neither the sphere of the infinity of space nor that of the infinity of consciousness, where there is neither perception nor non-perception. This is the end of suffering.[91]

But in passages like this there arises for the Western reader a very serious logical or epistemological problem. If, as the Buddha says, there are two regions or "realms", firstly the realm of "dependent co-arising" or of a clinging to the world and secondly the realm of nirvana, on entering which we leave every "I"-consciousness and every perception behind us, how could the Buddha possibly have reported to as-yet-unawakened men about the state he had attained to, since he overcame his consciousness of self on attaining to it? Just who or what was it that had undergone the "nirvana experience" in this state which was by definition "without consciousness"? Who or what was it that had memorized the form and nature of this "realm"? Or, to put it conversely, if every "I"-related experience has arisen only "co-dependently" with other factors and therefore has no being in itself, and if this "I"-related experience has been definitively surmounted by the leaving-behind of all attachments, then what "I" has survived these developments sufficiently to be able to report on them later? The Buddha himself paid no attention to this logical or epistemological incompatibility because it seemed to him to be an unimportant matter in relation to the actual salvationary practice which primarily concerned him. He speaks of the two "realms" as if their existence were self-evident:

I am skilled in this world and in the other world, [...] skilled in the realm of death and what is outside the realm of death. It will lead

to the welfare and happiness [...] of those who think they should listen to me and place faith in me.[92]

Buddhists of later centuries attempted to solve the "two-world" problem by ceasing to understand nirvana as a total extinction and to conceive of it rather as a sort of subject-less mental or spiritual state which would allow the recalling of experiences undergone in it but which would no longer involve the ascription of these experiences to an evaluating "I" or "mine". This would mean that, while there would still be perceptions in nirvana, they would not be referred back to any sense of self. It would be, so to speak, a matter of a perception without central point of focus. The contradiction consisting in the fact that the

Buddha was, on the one hand, in nirvana in a state of non-perception and of non-self but, on the other hand, could later, as Gautama Buddha, personally recall this experience is at least partially resolved if one bears in mind that this passage into nirvana meant that the Buddha passed into an "objective condition of mind" which he never lost or gave up even after his return to the world of "dependent co-arising" – something which we can conclude from the fact of his inspired and selfless thinking and acting even once "back in the world". It has also been argued by later Buddhists that the two "worlds" or "realms" referred to when the Buddha speaks of "awakening", in the nirvana experience, from the everyday world of "samsara" only appear to be, but are not really, separate from one another, since although "awakening" in nirvana does indeed constitute an overcoming of the "I", this "I" had in any case already beforehand existed only as an illusion. That is to say, neither in the "awoken" state of nirvana nor in the everyday world of "samsara" is there, in reality, any "I".

But in the last analysis the doctrine of Buddhism is simply not one to which the strict and exact criteria of philosophical coherence can be, or needs to be, applied. The Buddha, indeed, himself admits that nirvana cannot be grasped with logic:

Truly, I have found the doctrine [...] which cannot be achieved through logical thought.[93]

The Buddha tends to describe nirvana only indirectly or negatively, generally by contrast to the ephemeral and changeable world of everyday experience as "unbecome, unfabricated, uncreated, deathless, and no longer subject to any change." The reason for this portrayal in negative terms is that it is impossible to describe nirvana in its core essence using positive terms, that is to say, using words simply and directly. But this does not mean that nirvana is not real. The reports of the experiences of Zen masters and their students show that there really can exist a "nirvana dimension". Zen Buddhism, indeed, a school which flourished mainly in China and Japan, even took as its specific task to place "Zazen", the achievement of the meditative state, of "awakening", in the very centre of Buddhist teaching. Starting from the classic lotus-position sitting meditation of the Buddha, the attempt is made in Zen to deliberately eliminate that double dualism of everyday life: on the one hand the dualism of mind and body, on the other that of "I"-consciousness and external world, i.e. subject and object.

If, for example, we experience hunger in our everyday life, we ascribe this feeling of hunger to the stomach, that is to say, to our body and use our mind to ponder what we should do to deal with it: whether there is food in the fridge or whether we should go to the supermarket or a snack bar. If we are overweight, we ponder whether we ought to get our body into a fitness studio to bring it back into shape. That is to say, we experience body and mind as separate things.

But in meditation body and mind meld, through the flow of breath, into a single thing. The dualism is removed – just as we no longer experience here the world around us as an alien or resistant "outside" but rather now as a part of ourselves. We cease both to want, as subject, to produce effects in this external world and likewise cease to suffer its effects on us. The reciprocal effect of "inside" on "outside" and "outside" on "inside" which we know from our day to day lives is brought completely to a standstill and to peace. The famous Zen master Dogen evokes this in the following terms: "A man who has achieved awakening is like the moon reflected in water. The water is not moved by the moon and the moon not made wet by the water."[94]

We can also understand the elimination of the dualisms in Zen meditation by reference to the Buddha's doctrine of "dependent co-arising". There is, argues the Buddha, nothing in the universe which exists just out of itself. Everything is conditioned by something else. The seed of a plant bears in itself, indeed, the bases for its later development; but it becomes a flower only conditionally: namely, on the condition that it falls on fertile soil and that there is sufficient rain and sun for photosynthesis to occur. We ourselves are also conditioned: namely, by our conception, by our genes, by all that we perceive with our six senses from the moment of our birth on; by our instincts, feelings and needs; by our parents, encounters, culture and language; by the history of our country; and finally by human evolution in its entirety and through the "stardust" of the "Big Bang" and the patterns in which it settles.

The profound experience that nothing individual in the universe exists just in and by itself, neither the things around us nor even we ourselves, is itself the experience of "awakening". In this state, consciousness knows no "I" nor "not-I". If one were to try to find an image to express it, this might be that of a clear, cloudless sky which displays no limit, no "inner" or "outer". Consciousness is in the "here and now", without there being either observer or object of observation.[95]

This experience of awakening continues to exert its effects beyond the phase of meditation and develops a transformative power. Those who have experienced it report that it makes possible a certain firmness and resolution in daily life and, in the longer term, a more concentrated, fully present, and yet at the same time more calm and composed stance.

In recent years actual scientific research has been conducted into this effect, this transformative power, of meditation. There have been proven actually to occur, in meditating test subjects, certain clear neuro-psychological changes.96 Moreover; Buddhist meditation techniques have by now frequently been successfully applied to the treatment of a series of depressive ailments and disturbances causing attacks of distress, pain or fear. Perhaps best-known, worldwide, is so-called MBCT, or Mindfulness-Based Stress Reduction. This was developed in 1979 by the American molecular biologist Kabat-Zinn who, after years of intensive study of Zen Buddhism, succeeded in combining together various mindfulness exercises drawn from breathing, sitting and movement meditation into a therapeutic process. By "re-training" in this way the brain develops neural connections and forms of perception which make it possible to overcome existing conditions of anxiety, distress, helplessness and lethargy. In the "Stress Reduction Clinic" which Kabat-Zinn founded in Massachusetts he has achieved astonishing success above all with patients suffering from chronic pain, distress and depression. After the therapeutic efficacy of these techniques was scientifically evaluated in various large studies and recognized to be significant, they gained worldwide recognition and came to be widely applied.[97]

Whereas Buddhist meditation was for a long time looked upon in the West as just some esoteric, mystical ritual, its efficacy is nowadays no longer contested even by scientific researchers. The Buddha recognized already two and a half thousand years ago the liberating and transforming effect of meditation and wished to teach it to his contemporaries. At the same time he urged his monks, who had already progressed so far as to attain the state of being "awoken", to remain modest in their daily contacts with other people:

Our conduct should be purified, clear and open, flawless and restrained, and we will not laud ourselves or disparage others on account of this purified conduct.[98]

But how is a Buddhist, or a layman who has begun to study and practice Buddhism, and who has succeeded through the "sinking into oneself" that is meditation to free himself from attachment and "clinging" to the world, to conduct himself if he is still obliged, the next day and every day, to go to work and earn his living like everyone else? Is the "sinking into oneself" of meditation, if it issues eventually into a "nirvana experience", really compatible with the leading of a normal, everyday life in the world? Here too, the Buddha offers a very concrete answer:

> Our bodily conduct, our mental conduct, our verbal conduct have been purified [...] We guard the doors of our sense faculties. We are moderate in eating, we are devoted to wakefulness, and we are possessed of mindfulness and full awareness.[99]

Moreover, "awakened ones" will, in awareness of the universality of suffering, feel loving empathy for all living beings. To be "awoken" means, in everyday life, to be able to live in a liberated way even in the midst of our own limitations and determining conditions, and to commit oneself to the liberation also of other living beings.

This specific way of living does not necessarily exclude a hard-working life in the normal sense. It is, indeed, easier for those who lead the lives of monks and, like the Buddha himself, travel from place to place with their begging bowls, or those who live in monasteries outside of all the usual social constrictions, to become "arhats" or "awakened ones". But throughout history it has proven possible also for farmers, noblemen, businessmen, artisans and even kings to affirm and embrace the Buddha's doctrine. Such people, for example, contributed to the foundation of three monasteries in which, in his old age, the Buddha liked to spend the rainy season. These people, who are still bound into the social processes of production but who are already making efforts to understand the Four Noble Truths and thus their own clinging to "dependent co-arising" are described by the Buddha as "worldly believers", inasmuch as they are making efforts but are still attached to desire. Those who have already begun to overcome their "clinging" to the world the Buddha calls "stream-enterers". These latter are, indeed, still weak and a good way removed from true "awakening" but they have already begun tentatively to enter the stream of the overcoming of attachment. They have a good chance of really successfully crossing this stream:

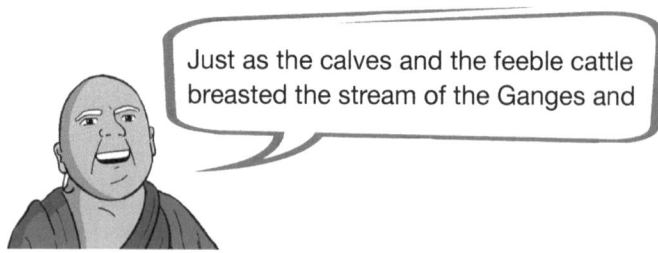

Just as the calves and the feeble cattle breasted the stream of the Ganges and got safely across to the farther shore, so too [...] the stream-enterers [...] will get safely across to the farther shore.[100]

The "stream-enterers", then, have indeed the aim of freeing themselves of all that is worldly and of attaining nirvana; nonetheless, they leave, at the end of their lives, mostly attachments and negative energies which must then be overcome by later generations in a series of rebirths, albeit a limited one. There are also "those who return but one time more". These are spirits who, in their last lives, had already completely freed themselves from attachment, hate, desire and blindness and are already in a position to attain nirvana. The Buddha names, then, with these four phrases "worldly believers", "stream-enterers", "those who return but one time more", and "arhats" four groups of people who are all seeking salvation but find themselves at different stages on the road to it.

This fact that the Buddha's doctrine integrates all human beings through their all being on the road to liberation, even if they are at different stages on it, opens up this doctrine beyond just the narrow confines of monastic life and draws in much wider social groups and strata.

In the last analysis, the Buddha urges all to follow the way he has followed, even if our life hitherto has been one of attachment and of greed. A businessman who was worried that too little time was left to him to follow the path of purity and awakening, given that he had already cheated so many people in his life, was reassured by the Buddha that even a very-few newly-grown branches suffice to make an old tree, when its time comes, fall in the right direction. Regardless of what we have done, it is never too late to turn around and to extinguish, through right action, wrong action:

> Someone who has succumbed to the taking of that which was not given can extinguish this by abstaining from the taking of that which was not given [...]

> Someone who has succumbed to untrue speech can extinguish this by abstaining from untrue speech.[101]

The Buddha's Legacy: Composure as Liberation and Radical Letting-Go

The Buddha's legacy is a dual one. One the one hand he taught that every human being should work, their whole life long, on their karma so as to leave no bad energies to the world that comes after them; on the other hand, however, he also taught that we should not overestimate ourselves. The French journalist and politician Clemenceau once said, we are told, that "the cemeteries of the world are full of people who considered themselves indispensable". These words might have been the Buddha's. Many human beings do in fact consider it to be the purpose of their lives to do nothing but work constantly at increasing their power, wealth and perceived importance. But in pursuing fame and recognition in this way they are succumbing to a great illusion. They take their life, their self and their part in the world to be considerably more significant than they actually are and push aside all thought of their actual nothingness. The Buddha reminds us of the ephemeral nature of all property and goods and indeed of the ephemeral nature of our own existence. He would surely also have rejected all our modern attempts to put off or slow down old age by "anti-ageing" techniques:

> Rather than living for a hundred years without recognizing the truth of ephemerality it is better to live just one day of knowledge regarding how all things arise and pass away.[102]

The Buddha reminds us always to follow the Middle Way: i.e. to neither surrender to the intoxication of the senses and to restless greed for external things nor turn away from the world completely, becoming totally ascetic and passive:

> Rise and set out at the right time upon the Way. If already as a young, strong, healthy man you are indolent, irresolute and mentally rigid, then you shall never find the Path of Understanding.[103]

The Buddha once explained the Middle Way to a player of a stringed instrument by using the simile of a "well-tuned string". One can give oneself over in life either to total asceticism or to total sensual self-indulgence. But just as the string of an instrument can only contribute to a beautiful sound if it is neither too tightly nor too loosely strung, likewise in life there must be sought out a way between the two extremes.[104]

But the Middle Way also means that we must accept life, and that each must do so at the particular place at which he finds himself in the world. The path to liberation from suffering through knowledge of the Four Noble Truths is one which stands, in principle, open to all human beings. Thus, there have always numbered among the Buddha's followers both men and women, farmers, businesspeople, people belonging to all the Indian castes and social strata. Of course, the Buddha concedes, it is easier for monks, who live retiring lives with few material needs, to withdraw from the material imperatives of this world and follow this path than it is for fathers or mothers of families. But a letting-go of the things of the world, and the achieving of a certain composure and extinction of the "I", is in principle possible for anyone. When someone returns out of the experience of meditation into everyday life he or she is able to perceive the external world with all its phenomena without succumbing to the illusion that it must all be centred upon and evaluated in relation to the "I":

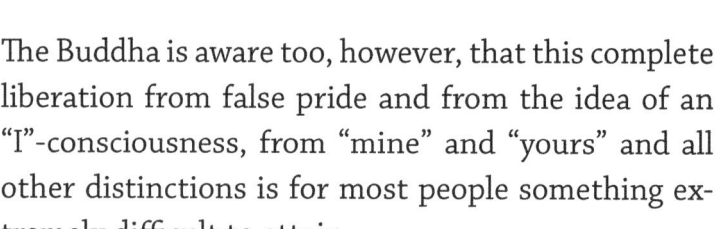

When one knows and sees thus, in regard to this body with consciousness and in regard to all external signs, the mind is rid of I-making, mine-making and conceit, has transcended discrimination, and is peaceful and well-liberated.[105]

The Buddha is aware too, however, that this complete liberation from false pride and from the idea of an "I"-consciousness, from "mine" and "yours" and all other distinctions is for most people something extremely difficult to attain.

Still today, just as in the Buddha's own day, we are far too tightly bound into the structures of "mine" and "yours", we acquire far too early in our lives a "sense of self" oriented to our social and economic successes and failures, for us ever to be able to let go of our "I"-consciousness altogether, let alone recognize this "I"-consciousness as fundamentally illusory. We are far too dependent on our needs for food and drink and sexual satisfaction, for a nice apartment, social recognition, a pension. Most people are so wrapped up in securing and increasing their life-chances and those of their children that they forget to even consider the ultimate meaning of their efforts and thus the meaning of life itself. There is also the fear of letting go, of no longer taking oneself seriously, and of possibly drifting thereby into a condition without will or drive. For this reason, we hold to what we are doing and what we have, wanting to keep and to increase it and tell ourselves that it will always remain as it is.

The Buddha, however, reminds us that our life is but the beat of a butterfly's wing in the vastness of time and that in the end nothing remains that we can take away with us from this life. We are, says the Buddha, in the end just thrown out of an eternal universe into existence, only to be dissolved once again after a short span of time. For this reason, we should not place our faith in material things. This message of the Buddha's is comforting but at the same time very sobering. Which of us really can, or really wants to, "let go"?

It is an interesting and fascinating development that for some decades now a greater and greater number of Buddha statues have been appearing above all in the households of large Western cities. Most people, indeed, who in such metropolises as London, Paris, Berlin or New York place, with decorative intent, a Buddha statue on their bookshelf or mantelpiece only have only a very vague idea of what the Buddha said or did. But when they are asked why they have a Buddha statue in their homes they are likely to reply that the statue is simply a beautiful object and emanates a beneficent aura of peace and composure. This is surely why such statues are also found in saunas, "wellness" hotels and such places. Just as Che Guevara has become an icon of revolution in the Western world, so has the Buddha become an icon of peace and mindfulness. This aestheticizing perception of the Buddha as the personification of peace and composure is indeed, at its core, not an entirely false one:

Abandoning restlessness and remorse, he abides unagitated with a mind inwardly peaceful.[106]

Such a perception of the Buddha, however, tends to overlook the way in which such an attitude is acquired. It arises, in fact, from an uncompromising radicalism. For the Buddha, there is no God and no life after death in any sort of "Paradise", however conceived. The eternal cycle of birth, life and death which we see occur in plants, animals, human beings and the entire universe is only a constant arrangement and re-arrangement of natural forces and energies. For the Buddha, indeed, there is not even an individual rebirth of the soul. Nor is the rebirth of positive karma energy an option. On the contrary: it is only if we succeed in leaving no negative energies behind us at our deaths that we attain the highest goal that we can attain, total extinction or nirvana:

I announce to you liberation from rebirth. There is now no longer any reason for desire for life. This is the end of suffering.[107]

The holy life is lived with nirvana as its ground, nirvana as its destination, nirvana as its final goal.[108]

If a person succeeds in adopting this mental and spiritual attitude of radical calm and composure, be it at the end of his life or already before this, it gives him the strength to cease to be disturbed by the heaviness of life and of death:

Once he has seen things in this way, his heart is freed from the driving of the senses. He understands: 'Birth is destroyed, the holy life has been lived, what had to be done has been done.'[109]

And as if this acceptance of the dissolution in nirvana were not the final farewell from all worldly striving, all fears and all inconstancy, the Buddha imparts to us, as he bids us farewell, one last steadying of our unquiet minds and spirits by assuring us that

[…] Beyond this, there is no longer anything any more.[110]

Bibliographical References

1   The Numerical Discourses of the Buddha, A Translation of the
    Angutara Nikkaya, by Bikkhu Bodhi, Wisdom Publications, Boston,
    2012, p. 202

2   The life of the Buddha cannot be dated precisely. The earliest
    calculations, made in what is now Sri Lanka, place his death in the
    year 544 BC, by Western reckoning, a date which still today, for most
    Buddhists, marks the beginning of their own calendar. This dating is
    now usually referred to by scholars as the "Southern Buddhist Chro-
    nology". In the latest research, however, historians and biographers
    have begun to proceed on the assumption that the Buddha's life lasted
    from circa 560 to circa 480 BC.

3   In the Buddha's Words, An Anthology of Discourses from the Pali
    Canon, edited and introduced by Bhikkhu Bodhi, Wisdom
    Publications, Boston, 2005, p. 214.

4   Ibid. p. 215.

5   Ibid. (translation slightly revised).

6   The Middle-Length Discourses of the Buddha: A New Translation of
    the Majjhima Nikaya, translated and edited by Bhikkhu Bodhi,
    Wisdom Publications, Boston, 1995, p. 260.

7   The Connected Discourses of the Buddha: A Translation of the
    Samyutta Nikaya, edited by Bhikkhu Bodhi, Wisdom Publications,
    Boston, 2000; Samyutta Nikaya 23.1, p. 984.

8   Ibid. p. 1846.

9   Ibid. p. 1844.

10 Ibid. p. 1845.

11 The Middle-Length Discourses of the Buddha: A New Translation of
    the Majjhima Nikaya, translated and edited by Bhikkhu Bodhi,
    Wisdom Publications, Boston, 1995 p. 261

12 Uddana VII, 1

13 Long Discourses of the Buddha: A Translation of the Digha Nikaya,
    translated by Maurice Walsh, Wisdom Publications, Boston, 1987,
    p. 243.

14 Ibid. p. 242.

15 Siddhartha Gautama is the Sanskrit form of his name. The older,
    Paliform is Siddhartha Gotama.

16 That there was indeed a real historical Buddha is by now a fact generally accepted both in Asia and in Europe. He had, indeed, been considered for many years by Europeans as merely a legendary or fictional figure. The Indologist Hermann Oldenburg (1854-1920), however, was the first European to exactly research the Buddha's life, to separate myth from reality, and to try to actually reconstruct the Buddha's biography. Since his work, even European scholars no longer doubt the Buddha's real existence. There are, indeed, still open questions regarding the exact dating and the full authenticity of the discourses and dialogues that have come down to us. Like Socrates and Confucius, the Buddha himself authored no books. His pupils, it is true, gathered together immediately after his death in a sort of council to sum up the teachings of their master and agree upon a faithful manner of expressing it. For a long time, however, the doctrine was passed on only orally. Thus, for example, various monks established, at this council, a canon of doctrine (Dharma) and a supplementary canon of rules for the monastic orders (Vinayapitaka), both of which were learned by heart. Only a century or so later did there arise, on this basis, the first written texts of Buddhism, composed in the Pali and Sanskrit languages. Buddha's own native language, however, had been neither of these languages but rather Magadhi, so that we must reckon with deviations in translation even in this initial phase. There then followed translations into Chinese and many other languages. The Pali Canon used in the present book is considered to be the earliest written record and thereby the most reliable source for the Buddha's actual pronouncements, although even here some later-added supplements must be taken into account. The Pali Canon consists of three "pikatas" (literally: of three "baskets"). This term was used because the texts were first written down on palm leaves which were then, once separated by theme, preserved in woven baskets. The first basket contained the Vinayapitaka, the rules for the monastic orders, the second the Suttas, the didactic speeches of the Master, and the third the Abhidhammapitakaya, the doctrine as schematically represented in the form of tables and lists. By far the most important and reliable of these sources is the "second basket", the Suttas, the real didactic discourses. These latter in their turn are divided into

various "collections", called "nikayas". We have the Digha Nikaya, the collection of longer discourses, the Majjhima Nikaya, the collection of the middle-length discourses, and the Samyutta Nikaya, the collection of the so-called "connected" discourses.

17 Buddha, Anguttara Nikaya, I, 1.

18 Ibid. IV, 104.

19 The Middle-Length Discourses of the Buddha: A New Translation of the Majjhima Nikaya, translated and edited by Bhikkhu Bodhi, Wisdom Publications, Boston, 1995, p. 256

20 Ibid. p. 339.

21 Ibid.

22 Ibid.

23 The Connected Discourses of the Buddha: A Translation of the Samyutta Nikaya, edited by Bhikkhu Bodhi, Wisdom Publications, Boston, 2000, p. 1350.

24 The Middle-Length Discourses of the Buddha: A New Translation of the Majjhima Nikaya, translated and edited by Bhikkhu Bodhi, Wisdom Publications, Boston, 1995, p. 259.

25 Ibid. p. 260.

26 Ibid. p. 264 (translation revised).

27 The Connected Discourses of the Buddha: A Translation of the Samyutta Nikaya, edited by Bhikkhu Bodhi, Wisdom Publications, Boston, 2000, p. 1844 (translation slightly revised).

28 Ibid.

29 In the Buddha's Words, An Anthology of Discourses from the Pali Canon, edited and introduced by Bhikkhu Bodhi, Wisdom Publications, Boston, 2005, p. 206 (translation revised).

30 The Middle-Length Discourses of the Buddha: A New Translation of the Majjhima Nikaya, translated and edited by Bhikkhu Bodhi, Wisdom Publications, Boston, 1995, p. 278.

31 Buddha, Udana: A Translation With Introduction and Notes by Thanissaro Bikkhu, Part I, 3, p. 28.

32 The Connected Discourses of the Buddha: A Translation of the Samyutta Nikaya, edited by Bhikkhu Bodhi, Wisdom Publications, Boston, 2000, p. 1349.

33 The Middle-Length Discourses of the Buddha: A New Translation of the Majjhima Nikaya, translated and edited by Bhikkhu Bodhi, Wisdom Publications, Boston, 1995, p. 266 (translation revised).

34 Buddha, Udana: A Translation With Introduction and Notes by Thanissaro Bikkhu, Part I, 3, p. 26. The Buddha speaks here of a "six sense-media" because he counts, in addition to the realms of seeing, hearing, touching, smelling and tasting, also that of thinking and the "organ of thought" among the realms of sense.

35 Ibid. p. 28.

36 Ibid. pp. 26 and 27.

37 Ibid. pp. 27 and 28.

38 The Middle-Length Discourses of the Buddha: A New Translation of the Majjhima Nikaya, translated and edited by Bhikkhu Bodhi, Wisdom Publications, Boston, 1995, p. 260 (translation revised).

39 The Connected Discourses of the Buddha: A Translation of the Samyutta Nikaya, edited by Bhikkhu Bodhi, Wisdom Publications, Boston, 2000, pp. 957-958.

40 Ibid. (translation revised).

41 Ibid. p. 1140.

42 The Middle-Length Discourses of the Buddha: A New Translation of the Majjhima Nikaya, translated and edited by Bhikkhu Bodhi, Wisdom Publications, Boston, 1995, p. 120.

43 The Connected Discourses of the Buddha: A Translation of the Samyutta Nikaya, edited by Bhikkhu Bodhi, Wisdom Publications, Boston, 2000, p. 541.

44 Buddha, Anguttara Nikaya, 4, 45.

45 The Middle-Length Discourses of the Buddha: A New Translation of the Majjhima Nikaya, translated and edited by Bhikkhu Bodhi, Wisdom Publications, Boston, 1995, p. 229-230.

46 Ibid. p. 260.

47 Ibid.

48 The Connected Discourses of the Buddha: A Translation of the Samyutta Nikaya, edited by Bhikkhu Bodhi, Wisdom Publications, Boston, 2000, p. 885 (translation revised). "Samsara" too, the beginning and end of which are unimaginable, must pass away for him who possesses true knowledge.

49 Buddha, Udana: A Translation With Introduction and Notes by Thanissaro Bikkhu, Part 8, I, p. 113.

50 The Middle-Length Discourses of the Buddha: A New Translation of the Majjhima Nikaya, translated and edited by Bhikkhu Bodhi, Wisdom Publications, Boston, 1995, p. 645

51   Ibid. p. 646.

52   Ibid. p. 232.

53   Ibid. p. 350.

54   The Connected Discourses of the Buddha: A Translation of the
      Samyutta Nikaya, edited by Bhikkhu Bodhi, Wisdom Publications,
      Boston, 2000, p. 1846.

55   Ibid. p. 1844.

56   The Middle-Length Discourses of the Buddha: A New Translation
      of the Majjhima Nikaya, translated and edited by Bhikkhu Bodhi,
      Wisdom Publications, Boston, 1995, pp. 448-49.

57   See Hans Wolfgang Schumann, Der Historische Buddha, Munich,
      1999.

58   The Middle-Length Discourses of the Buddha: A New Translation
      of the Majjhima Nikaya, translated and edited by Bhikkhu Bodhi,
      Wisdom Publications, Boston, 1995, pp. 120-21.

59   Ibid.

60   Ibid. pp. 222-23.

61   The Connected Discourses of the Buddha: A Translation of the
      Samyutta Nikaya, edited by Bhikkhu Bodhi, Wisdom Publications,
      Boston, 2000, p. 698-99.

62   The Middle-Length Discourses of the Buddha: A New Translation
      of the Majjhima Nikaya, translated and edited by Bhikkhu Bodhi,
      Wisdom Publications, Boston, 1995, pp. 267-68 (translation revised).

63   The Long Discourses of the Buddha, A Translation by Maurice Walshe,
      Wisdom Publications, Boston, 1987, p.189.

64   Ibid. p. 190.

65   Ibid. p. 178.

66   Ibid.

67   Ibid.

68   The Connected Discourses of the Buddha: A Translation of the
      Samyutta Nikaya, edited by Bhikkhu Bodhi, Wisdom Publications,
      Boston, 2000, p. 875.

69   The Middle-Length Discourses of the Buddha: A New Translation
      of the Majjhima Nikaya, translated and edited by Bhikkhu Bodhi,
      Wisdom Publications, Boston, 1995, pp. 260-61.

70   The Connected Discourses of the Buddha: A Translation of the
      Samyutta Nikaya, edited by Bhikkhu Bodhi, Wisdom Publications,

Boston, 2000, p. 914.

71 Ibid. p. 882. Samsara too, the beginning and end of which are beyond comprehension, must pass away for the person who possesses true knowledge.

72 The Middle-Length Discourses of the Buddha: A New Translation of the Majjhima Nikaya, translated and edited by Bhikkhu Bodhi, Wisdom Publications, Boston, 1995, p. 228.

73 Ibid.

74 Ibid.

75 The saying is from the 9th-century Buddhist monk Linji Yixuan.

76 The Middle-Length Discourses of the Buddha: A New Translation of the Majjhima Nikaya, translated and edited by Bhikkhu Bodhi, Wisdom Publications, Boston, 1995, p. 256.

77 Thich Nhat Hanh, like the Dalai Lama, has also been a prominent ambassador for the Buddhist doctrine to the West. An advocate of a "politically committed Buddhism", he helps and promotes, through books, lectures, political initiatives, and meditation seminars, not only access to the "nirvana experience" but also a very modern and universal Buddhistic vision of ethical action and orientation. He links the doctrine of the Buddha with ways of solving contemporary problems of social and political justice.

78 The Middle-Length Discourses of the Buddha: A New Translation of the Majjhima Nikaya, translated and edited by Bhikkhu Bodhi, Wisdom Publications, Boston, 1995, p. 145.

79 Ibid.

80 Ibid. p. 146.

81 Ibid. p. 149-50.

82 Ibid. p. 146.

83 Ibid. p. 149

84 Ibid. p. pp. 250-51.

85 Ibid. pp. 251-52.

86 Buddha, Iti Vuttaka, II, 6.

87 Ibid.

88 Ludwig Wittgenstein, Tractatus Logico-Philosophicus

89 René Descartes, Discourse on Method.

90 Buddha, Udana: A Translation With Introduction and Notes by Thanissaro Bikkhu, Part VIII, p. 113.

91 Ibid. (translation revised).

92 The Middle-Length Discourses of the Buddha: A New Translation
   of the Majjhima Nikaya, translated and edited by Bhikkhu Bodhi,
   Wisdom Publications, Boston, 1995, p. 320.

93 Ibid. p. 257 (translation revised).

94 Master Dogen Shobogenzo, Treasury of the True Dharma Eye.

95 See Gert Scobel, Achtsamkeit und die Transformation von Koerper,
   Berlin, 2018.

96 Recent research has proven, for example, that those who meditate
   regularly come to display, among other morphological changes, a
   higher density of nerve-cells in the orbito-frontal cortex. Changes in
   EEG activity have also been measured.

97 The following two meta-studies from 2010 and 2011, in particular,
   have shown that the psychological sufferings of the chronically ill can
   be successfully treated using MBSR: Ernst Bohlmeijer et al, The Effects
   of Mindfulness-Based Stress Reduction Therapy on Mental Health of
   Adults With a Chronic Mental Disease, in Journal of Psychosomatic
   Research 68, pp. 539-544, Entschede 2010; and Lone Fjorback et al,
   Mindfulness-Based Stress Reduction and Mindfulness-Based Cogni-
   tive Therapy in Acta Psychiatrica Scandinavica 124 (2) pp. 102-119,
   Aarhus, 2011.

98 The Middle-Length Discourses of the Buddha: A New Translation
   of the Majjhima Nikaya, translated and edited by Bhikkhu Bodhi,
   Wisdom Publications, Boston, 1995, p. 363.

99 Ibid. p. 366.

100 Ibid. p. 321.

101 Ibid. p. 131.

102 Buddha, Dhammapada 113.

103 Ibid.

104 See Pali Vinaya Mahavagga, V.

105 The Connected Discourses of the Buddha: A Translation of the
    Samyutta Nikaya, edited by Bhikkhu Bodhi, Wisdom Publications,
    Boston, 2000, p. 699.

106 The Middle-Length Discourses of the Buddha: A New Translation
    of the Majjhima Nikaya, translated and edited by Bhikkhu Bodhi,
    Wisdom Publications, Boston, 1995, p. 366.

107 Buddha, Udana: A Translation With Introduction and Notes by
    Thanissaro Bikkhu, Part VIII, p. 115.

108 The Connected Discourses of the Buddha: A Translation of the

Samyutta Nikaya, edited by Bhikkhu Bodhi, Wisdom Publications, Boston, 2000, p. 985.

109 The Middle-Length Discourses of the Buddha: A New Translation of the Majjhima Nikaya, translated and edited by Bhikkhu Bodhi, Wisdom Publications, Boston, 1995, p. 122.

110 Ibid. (translation revised).

Already published in the same series:

Walther Ziegler
Adorno in 60 Minutes
ISBN 9783750460232

Walther Ziegler
Arendt in 60 Minutes
ISBN 9783752649031

Walther Ziegler
Camus in 60 Minutes
ISBN 9783741227738

Walther Ziegler
Confucius in 60 Minutes
ISBN 9783753423128

Walther Ziegler
Foucault in 60 Minutes
ISBN 978375342688

Walther Ziegler
Freud in 60 Minutes
ISBN 9783741227707

Walther Ziegler
Habermas in 60 Minutes
ISBN 9783752612370

Walther Ziegler
Hegel in 60 Minutes
ISBN 9783741227677

Walther Ziegler
Heidegger in 60 Minutes
ISBN 9783741227752

Walther Ziegler
Hobbes in 60 Minutes
ISBN 9783751968317

Walther Ziegler
Kant in 60 Minutes
ISBN 9783741226373

Walther Ziegler
Marx in 60 Minutes
ISBN 9783741227691

Walther Ziegler
Nietzsche in 60 Minutes
ISBN 9783752803822

Walther Ziegler
Rawls in 60 Minutes
ISBN 9783750424050

Walther Ziegler
Rousseau in 60 Minutes
ISBN 9783741227622

Walther Ziegler
Sartre in 60 Minutes
ISBN 9783741227653

Walther Ziegler
Smith in 60 Minutes
ISBN 9783741227721

Walther Ziegler
Platon in 60 Minutes
ISBN 9783741227615

Walther Ziegler
Popper in 60 Minutes
ISBN 9783750470897

Walther Ziegler
Schopenhauer in 60 Minutes
ISBN 9783750498853

Walther Ziegler
Wittgenstein in 60 Minutes
ISBN 9783750426955

The author:

Dr Walther Ziegler is academically trained in the fields of philosophy, history and political science. As a foreign correspondent, reporter and newsroom coordinator for the German TV station ProSieben he has produced films on every continent. His news reports have won several prizes and awards. He has also authored numerous books in the field of philosophy. His many years of experience as a journalist mean that he is able to present the complex ideas of the great philosophers in a way that is both engaging and very clear. Since 2007 he has also been active as a teacher and trainer of young TV journalists in Munich, holding the post of Academic Director at the Media Academy, a University of Applied Sciences that offers film and TV courses at its base directly on the site of the major European film production company Bavaria Film. After the huge success of the book series "Great thinkers in 60 Minutes", he works as a freelance writer and philosopher.